Forest School and Autism

T0385404

of related interest

Listening to Young Children, Expanded Third Edition
A Guide to Understanding and Using the Mosaic Approach
Alison Clark
Foreword by Peter Moss
ISBN 978 1 90939 122 2
eISBN 978 1 90939 126 0

Living Sensationally
Understanding Your Senses
Winnie Dunn
ISBN 978 1 84310 871 9 (Hardback)
ISBN 978 1 84310 915 0 (Paperback)
eISBN 978 1 84642 733 6

Exercising Muscles and Minds
Outdoor Play and the Early Years Curriculum
Marjorie Ouvry
ISBN 978 1 90478 701 3
eISBN 978 1 90796 925 6

A Practical Guide to Happiness in Children
and Teens on the Autism Spectrum
A Positive Psychology Approach
Victoria Honeybourne
ISBN 978 1 78592 347 0
eISBN 978 1 78450 681 0

Forest School and Autism

A PRACTICAL GUIDE

MICHAEL JAMES

Jessica Kingsley *Publishers*
London and Philadelphia

First published in 2018
by Jessica Kingsley Publishers
73 Collier Street
London N1 9BE, UK
and
400 Market Street, Suite 400
Philadelphia, PA 19106, USA

www.jkp.com

Copyright © Michael James 2018

All rights reserved. No part of this publication may be reproduced in any
material form (including photocopying, storing in any medium by electronic
means or transmitting) without the written permission of the copyright owner
except in accordance with the provisions of the law or under terms of a licence
issued in the UK by the Copyright Licensing Agency Ltd. www.cla.co.uk or in
overseas territories by the relevant reproduction rights organisation, for details
see www.ifrro.org. Applications for the copyright owner's written permission to
reproduce any part of this publication should be addressed to the publisher.

Warning: The doing of an unauthorised act in relation to a copyright work
may result in both a civil claim for damages and criminal prosecution.

Library of Congress Cataloging in Publication Data
A CIP catalog record for this book is available from the Library of Congress

British Library Cataloguing in Publication Data
A CIP catalogue record for this book is available from the British Library

ISBN 978 1 78592 291 6
eISBN 978 1 78450 595 0

Printed and bound in Great Britain

For Joseph, because he loved the woods.

Contents

Acknowledgements

I would like to thank Andrew James and Jessica Kingsley Publishers for the opportunity to write this book.

Thanks to the people who read through chapters for me and offered invaluable advice: Emma Giffard, Alister Hillman, Alison Oldfield, Julia Butler and Alex Blake.

Thanks most of all to my children, Ossie and Mari, and to all the South West site community.

Introduction

I should begin with a confession. I'm not a writer. I have spent the last 16 years supporting autistic people in various settings. I have worked with all kinds of people, of all ages and abilities. I have a passion for my work and one of the aspects I have loved most is creating opportunities for the people I've supported.

I have always been an outdoors type of person and several years ago I volunteered to help at a Forest School session which my son, Ossie, attended through his school. It was great fun and I immediately saw an opportunity to contribute myself. I completed my Forest School training and began running sessions. My work with Forest School has been very well received by professionals and has gained recognition, with a finalist's place in the Autism Category at a national award ceremony, a request to give a presentation at an international conference and the opportunity to write this book. Most importantly, I have seen the way that Forest School has benefited the people who participate in my sessions.

This is not an academic book. I am not qualified to write that type of book. This book offers practical advice, learned over many years. During a recent session, a support worker said that I have the 'magic touch' with the people we support. There is no magic, just basic autism awareness and experience of how to apply it, and I attempt to share that knowledge in this book.

I hope that this book helps people who have an interest in autism to consider Forest School as one of the opportunities that can be offered to people with autism spectrum disorders. I also hope that this book offers simple and practical advice to Forest School leaders and other outdoor education practitioners, which will help them to create autism-inclusive opportunities in their respective settings.

Most of all, I hope that this book is not the last word on autism and Forest School, but rather part of a conversation about how outdoor education can develop autism-inclusive practice.

CHAPTER 1

What is Forest School?

All across the UK there is something happening in the woods. If you follow the track down into the shade of the trees, there is a good chance you may discover clusters of dens made out of fallen branches. Wander a little further and you may see a fire pit with a square of logs arranged around it. You might be forgiven for thinking that you've stumbled on the Ewok village. What is this all about?

Perhaps, if you happen along at the right time, there'll be a group of people there; they'll probably be busying around and looking as if they're having fun, but if you stop to ask them what they're doing then chances are they'll reply 'Forest School'.

So what is Forest School?

Forest School is a type of inspirational teaching that takes learners into natural settings with an emphasis on experiential learning and building confidence and self-esteem. Forest School aims to promote the holistic development of everyone involved, including the practitioners, in a person-centred way.

Forest School was introduced to the UK by early years practitioners from Bridgwater College who travelled to Denmark to observe Danish early years methods. They found a culture of taking children into the outdoors throughout the seasons ('frulitsliv') and returned to the UK inspired to incorporate the Danish model into their own practice. In 1995, Bridgwater College began to offer courses in Forest School. Initially the focus was on early years practitioners but as Forest School started to spread, it began to be offered to participants of all ages.

Although the term Forest School is comparatively new, the ethos behind it should be seen as part of the wider tradition of outdoor education that has been long established around the world. Perhaps the most famous example of this tradition is the Scout Association, which began in 1907 and grew into an international movement that is still going strong today.

Building on these traditions Forest School has been very successful in the UK, experiencing phenomenal exponential growth since its beginnings in the mid-1990s.

Forest Schools can now be found all around the world. In the United States (US), there is increasing interest in Forest Schools and in nature schools. Between 2012 and 2016 there has been a six-fold increase in the number of nature-based pre-schools.[1] Interest in Forest School for pre-school children in the US is being encouraged by media interest, and the article 'Preschool Without Walls' published in the *New York Times* was very widely shared.[2] As interest grows it seems very possible that Forest School may begin to take hold in the US in the same way it has in the UK.

In 2012, the Forest School Association (FSA) was established in the UK to promote cohesion and best practice. The FSA produces the Criteria for Best Practice, which explains the principles that underlie the Forest School ethos.

Principles and criteria for good practice

Principle 1: Forest School is a long-term process of frequent and regular sessions in a woodland or natural environment, rather than a one-off visit. Planning, adaptation, observations and reviewing are integral elements of Forest School.

* Forest School takes place regularly, ideally at least every other week, with the same group of learners, over an extended period of time, if practicable encompassing the seasons.

* A Forest School programme has a structure which is based on the observations and collaborative work between learners

and practitioners. This structure should clearly demonstrate progression of learning.

* The initial sessions of any programme establish physical and behavioural boundaries as well as making initial observations on which to base future programme development.

Principle 2: Forest School takes place in a woodland or natural wooded environment to support the development of a relationship between the learner and the natural world.

* While woodland is the ideal environment for Forest School, many other sites, some with only a few trees, are able to support good Forest School practice.

* The woodland is ideally suited to match the needs of the programme and the learners, providing them with the space and environment in which to explore and discover.

* A Forest School programme constantly monitors its ecological impact and works within a sustainable site management plan agreed between the landowner/manager, the Forest School practitioner and the learners.

* Forest School aims to foster a relationship with nature through regular personal experiences in order to develop long-term, environmentally sustainable attitudes and practices in staff, learners and the wider community.

* Forest School uses natural resources for inspiration, to enable ideas and to encourage intrinsic motivation.

Principle 3: Forest School aims to promote the holistic development of all those involved, fostering resilient, confident, independent and creative learners.

* Where appropriate, the Forest School leader will aim to link experiences at Forest School to home, work and/or school education.

* Forest School programmes aim to develop, where appropriate, the physical, social, cognitive, linguistic, emotional, social and spiritual aspects of the learner.

Principle 4: Forest School offers learners the opportunity to take supported risks appropriate to the environment and to themselves.

* Forest School opportunities are designed to build on an individual's innate motivation, positive attitudes and/or interests.

* Forest School uses tools and fires only where deemed appropriate to the learners, and dependent on completion of a baseline risk assessment.

* Any Forest School experience follows a risk–benefit process managed jointly by the practitioner and learner that is tailored to the developmental stage of the learner.

Principle 5: Forest School is run by qualified Forest School practitioners who continuously maintain and develop their professional practice.

* Forest School is led by qualified Forest School practitioners, who are required to hold a minimum of an accredited Level 3 Forest School qualification.

* There is a high ratio of practitioners/adults to learners.

* Practitioners and adults regularly helping at Forest School are subject to relevant checks into their suitability to have prolonged contact with children, young people and vulnerable people.

* Practitioners need to hold an up-to-date first-aid qualification, which includes paediatric (if appropriate) and outdoor elements.

* Forest School is backed by relevant working documents, which contain all the policies and procedures required for running Forest School and which establish the roles and responsibilities of staff and volunteers.

    ★   The Forest School leader is a reflective practitioner and sees themselves, therefore, as a learner too.

Principle 6: Forest School uses a range of learner-centred processes to create a community for development and learning.

    ★   A learner-centred pedagogical approach is employed by Forest School that is responsive to the needs and interests of learners.

    ★   The Practitioner models the pedagogy, which they promote during their programmes through careful planning, appropriate dialogue and relationship building.

    ★   Play and choice are an integral part of the Forest School learning process, and play is recognised as vital to learning and development at Forest School.

    ★   Forest School provides a stimulus for all learning preferences and dispositions.

    ★   Reflective practice is a feature of each session to ensure that learners and practitioners can understand their achievements, develop emotional intelligence and plan for the future.

    ★   Practitioner observation is an important element of Forest School pedagogy. Observations feed into 'scaffolding' and tailoring experiences to learning and development at Forest School.

Forest School is accessed through schools, nurseries and day centres as well as directly from private providers and is in no way confined to rural areas. You are just as likely to stumble across the signs of a Forest School in a copse in a city park as you are in the countryside, and the Forest School idea has given birth to Beach Schools along the coast.

It is a common misconception that Forest School activities are basically Bear Grylls for kids. In fact, sessions develop around the learners and can involve social development, crafts, science, numeracy, practical skills, music, drama…and anything you can think of! The key elements of the process are that it takes place in a natural setting and is led by the learners.

Research evidences a wide range of benefits provided by regular time spent in natural settings, including increased confidence, greater emotional well-being, increased concentration, physical fitness, improvement in fine and gross motor skills and better social skills.[3]

The bestselling book *Last Child in the Woods* by Richard Louv (2010)[4] coined the phrase 'nature deficit disorder' to describe the worrying symptoms, such as obesity, depression and attention disorders, that seem to increase as children spend less time playing outdoors. As awareness of the benefits to well-being associated with getting out into the woods has grown, so Forest Schools have flourished.

At the time of writing, the Forest School programme is delivered to thousands of people across the UK. Participants come from all backgrounds, and in some cases Forest School provides the only opportunity for people to access nature. Estimates suggest that one in a hundred people in the UK has autism[5] and autistic people, of all ages and abilities, are attending Forest School in increasing numbers. As one participant's parent put it, 'Forest school is a very important part of his life, he really does enjoy it.'

This book will discuss how to develop an autism-aware approach to Forest School practice and explain how this benefits all participants.

CHAPTER 2

What is Autism?

Most people have heard the term autism and know that it relates to a condition that impairs a person's ability to communicate with others. Unfortunately, many people's understanding of what this actually means is vague, and negative assumptions and misconceptions persist.

Autism describes a developmental condition that affects a person's ability to interact with others and how they perceive the world around them. Autism is a spectrum condition, which means that although autistic people will share some level of impairment in similar areas, their autism will affect them in different ways.

At one end of the spectrum, autistic people may have significant learning disabilities and require 24-hour support in order to lead their lives, while at the other end the person may be very intelligent and successful in their chosen career but require a little support and understanding from others in some areas of their life. The experience of many autistic people will lie somewhere between these two points. From the point of view of a professional wishing to provide a service directly to an autistic person, the key is to develop an understanding of that person as an individual.

This chapter is only intended as an introduction to autism. There is a great deal of literature available in print and online that covers the subject in detail. I would include the caveat that a little bit of theory can be a dangerous thing! An understanding of theory is very important if you want to increase your awareness of autism but be conscious of how you apply it to an individual. Do not try to force a template you've formed from a basic understanding of theory onto someone. If it doesn't fit you will only create assumptions about that person that may prove counterproductive. Always put the person at the centre of your practice.

Diagnostic criteria

In order to be diagnosed with autism a person must meet diagnostic criteria. There are different diagnostic criteria and but there are two that are most commonly used.

The *International Classification of Diseases, tenth edition (ICD-10)* is the manual used in the UK. The *ICD-10* lists different profiles relating to autism under the title Pervasive Developmental Disorders, which can be described as a group of disorders which affect an individual's ability in social interaction and communication and a narrow, repetitive range of interests and activities with these differences being present in all situations.

These profiles include childhood autism, Asperger syndrome and atypical autism and reflect the understanding of autism as a spectrum condition and the breadth of difference in how autism presents in individual people.

The *Diagnostic and Statistical Manual, fifth edition (DSM-5)* is the American manual, which was updated in 2013. Changes were made in the description of diagnostic criteria in an attempt to simplify terminology, and behaviours associated with differences in sensory processing were included. Different autistic profiles, such as Asperger syndrome or PDD-NOS (pervasive developmental disorder – not otherwise specified), are no longer used and are replaced by the term autism spectrum disorder.

The manual describes autism spectrum disorder as impacting on the individual's abilities in social communication and social interaction and the individual displaying restricted and repetitive interests or behaviour. These differences will have been observed since early childhood and will be significant enough to impair day-to-day living.

Diagnosis includes specifiers that describe the amount of support an individual requires, and recognises that this may fluctuate over the course of someone's life.

In addition, *DSM-5* describes a new condition, social (pragmatic) communication disorder, which is identified as being distinct from autism. Similar impairments in social communication are presented but repetitive patterns of behaviour and narrow interests are not present.

ICD-10 is due to be updated in 2018 and it is expected that it will be influenced by the changes made to *DSM-5*.

This is only the latest change in how autism is diagnosed and is partly a response to the last significant change to diagnosis when the concept of a spectrum was introduced.[1]

In 1994, *DSM-IV* included Asperger syndrome as a new clinical diagnosis and this led to a great surge in the number of people being diagnosed with autism. Current research suggests that a great many people present autistic traits and that there is no clear cut-off point between people at the most functional end of the spectrum and the general population.[2]

Difficulties in social communication and interaction

DSM-IV described differences in social communication and social interaction as two distinct categories, with repetitive patterns of behaviour making a third category (a triad). *DSM-5* describes autism in terms of a dyad of impairment and seeks to move away from the triad model by including social communication and interaction in one category, with the other category being repetitive behaviours and restricted interests.

Social communication

Communication is the message that is sent or received. Typical social communication uses verbal language, tone of voice, body language and facial expression. Autistic people experience difficulty in processing received communication and in expressing themselves to others.

Autistic people tend to take things which are said literally and may not understand figures of speech or metaphor. Neurotypical people may say words which mean one thing but they change the meaning using body language and tone of voice.[3] This is sometimes done to try to convey meaning in a gentler way, sometimes to be sarcastic, but is very confusing to someone who cannot pick up the signals that are being conveyed along with the words. Autistic people usually prefer direct, literal communication and this can come across as abrupt or rude to people who are not used to it.

Some autistic people may have very limited verbal language and others may use verbal language in idiosyncratic ways, such as repeating back what others have said or liking others to repeat back what they have said, or using a limited repertoire of phrases to express themselves.

Some autistic people may present a delay in processing verbal information and find simpler sentences easier to understand.

Social interaction

Social interaction is the reciprocal exchange of communication between people. Autistic people experience difficulty in reading other people and navigating social situations. Neurotypical people tend to frame their social interactions using subtle hints which are communicated using body language and tone of voice. If you have trouble picking up these hints it becomes difficult to know when it is your turn to speak, when someone is trying to begin or end a conversation with you or whether they are expressing emotion in what they are saying.

Autistic people may also find it difficult to use their own body language and tone of voice in the ways that neurotypical people expect. They may give eye contact at the wrong times and for longer or shorter periods than expected or sometimes find it hard to make eye contact at all. They may find it hard to judge personal space and may misinterpret physical contact.

Autistic people may find it difficult to show a polite interest in others if they aren't actually interested and may have a tendency to want to speak about their own interests and not pick up hints that the people they are talking to would like to move the conversation away from this.

When Lorna Wing described the triad of impairment she described social interaction and social communication as two separate categories and went on to describe social imagination as the third part of the triad.

Social imagination

This describes the difficulty which autistic people have in understanding other people's perspectives. The ability to understand and predict other people's feelings and actions is called Theory of Mind. Autistic people may have trouble in the extent to which they can do this, which leads on to finding new situations hard to cope with and finding it hard to predict what could be happening next. Autistic people may find it hard to play interpersonal games that focus on playing out imagined roles in an improvised way.

Difficulty in this area can cause significant stress for a person as they can find themselves unable to find their bearings in a situation in the way that a neurotypical person can.

Restricted and repetitive patterns of behaviours, activities or interests

Autistic people may have a reliance on fixed routines and structure and find sudden changes difficult to cope with. They may seek predictable situations and sameness in their lives and show a level of rigidity in how they pursue this. There may be a reluctance to try new things, even if they appear to others to be something which they would expect the person to enjoy.

The repetitive behaviours of some autistic people can seem eccentric to other people and cause them to stand out. Sometimes these behaviours may involve repetitive actions to stimulate the senses, such as hand flapping; sometimes they may involve wanting always to have a favourite object with them or wear a particular item of clothing.

Autistic people may have hobbies or interests that they focus on intently. These interests are very important to people and the opportunity to enjoy them is vital for their well-being. These interests should not be described as obsessive unless they interfere with a person's ability to live their day-to-day life.

Sensory processing

The majority of autistic people present a level of difference in sensory processing which affects them in their day-to-day lives.[4] This can be experienced in the processing of one of the senses or can occur across more than one sense simultaneously. Sometimes this may present as being over-sensitive to stimuli and sometimes under-sensitive. In some cases, sensory perception may be experienced in very intense ways – people's field of vision can appear fractured as if looking at shattered glass or people may be experiencing synaesthesia, where stimulation of one of the senses triggers a sensation in another.

We perceive the world and our place in it using seven senses:

- visual: sense of sight

- auditory: sense of hearing

- olfactory: sense of smell

- tactile: sense of touch

- gustatory: sense of taste

- vestibular: sense of balance

- proprioception: sense of our physical positioning and the strength of effort our body is exerting.

Differences in processing these senses can have a profound effect on a person. Over-sensitivity to stimuli (hypersensitivity) can cause irritation or sometimes trigger fear and anxiety. The senses can become overwhelmed with sensory input to the degree that a person cannot cope. The National Autistic Society recently produced a short film called *Too Much Information*, which can be found on YouTube. The film shows the experience of walking through a busy shopping mall from the perspective of an autistic child experiencing an overload of sensory information. I would recommend taking a moment to watch this film if you have never experienced sensory overload personally.

If people are under-sensitive to stimuli (hyposensitivity) they may need to engage in behaviours to seek the sensation they are lacking, such as rocking their bodies. These behaviours may appear odd to other people and the strong need to create them can prevent someone from focusing on the other things that are happening around them.

Sensory processing differences can cause some people more difficulties than any of the other aspects of their autism, particularly if efforts have not been made to understand and make accommodations for them.

The diagnostic criteria describe how autism appears to others. There are different theories as to why autism affects a person in the way that it does. Science has not yet come up with a single unifying theory that explains autism. Currently, research shows a genetic disposition towards developing autism, which may be influenced by environmental factors.

Executive function

Executive function is the term that describes the cognitive processes which regulate, control and manage our thoughts and actions. It is our brain's control room.

Autistic people display differences in how their brains carry out executive functions and these differences vary from person to person.

Executive function can be broken down into different components, which can be put into two groups: organisation functions and regulation functions.

Organisation functions

Planning – This is the ability to evaluate different options, choose the best ones then organise and sequence them to reach a goal. Planning not only describes marshalling your thoughts but also applies to learning sequences of physical movements.

Problem solving – This is the ability to identify and overcome obstacles. In order to solve problems, we need to be flexible in our thinking and be able to find different angles to approach our problem from. We need to have nuanced thinking and see that a situation may have grey areas. Autistic people often find this difficult and may see a situation as 'all or nothing' and struggle to change course and consider alternatives.

Verbal reasoning – This is the ability to understand and evaluate concepts as they are described in words. An autistic person may understand the words used but may take them literally and find it difficult to understand different meanings being conveyed by the same word when it is used in different contexts or spoken in different tones.

Working memory – This is the ability to hold things in our short-term memory while we complete another task. Autistic people may find it easier to to focus on one thing at a time and may struggle to multi-task.

Attention – This is the ability to focus on a task or social interaction. It involves filtering out other input from your thoughts or the environment around you. Some autistic people struggle to focus their attention on the things which other people expect them to.

Action functions

Inhibition – This is the ability to suppress thoughts or actions. This may be the suppression of thoughts, emotions or impulses that enter our minds when we are trying to focus on something else. Autistic people may find it hard not to become overwhelmed by emotions, they may struggle to resist a pleasurable activity or to stop the activity once they've started and, in some cases, may be impulsive.

Initiation of actions – This is the ability to begin a task and involves the step between thinking and doing. Some autistic people find it hard to take this step and may require some form of prompt to begin a task.

Monitoring of actions – This is the ability to keep an activity on track. It's a little like our brain's autopilot. When we learn a task, we need to consciously monitor how we are carrying out the activity but as we learn the skill, much of this can be carried out subconsciously and we can think of something else while we do it. This helps us to generalise the activity. Autistic people may find it difficult to generalise an experience and apply it to different settings or contexts.

Cognitive flexibility – This is the ability to shift attention in response to change. Autistic people may find it difficult to change their minds when they receive new information. This can cause difficulty in making the transition from one activity to another or in seeing different aspects of the same subject simultaneously.

We can see that these functions are interconnected and a difference in how one is operating is likely to impact on others. As well as direct neurological differences in how the brain is carrying out these functions, these different abilities may also be impacted on by factors such as sensory processing. It would be extremely difficult to maintain attention and monitor actions if you were subject to overwhelming sensory input. Imagine trying to follow an unfamiliar knitting pattern with your head in the bass speaker at a rock concert or with an army of ants crawling across your back.

Central coherence

Central coherence is the ability to step back and see the bigger picture. Autistic people show a tendency to be very focused on the details in a situation but do not always see the bigger picture. Uta Frith put forward the 'weak central coherence theory' in the 1980s, which suggested that autistic people typically tend to process everything at a local level. Research[5] now suggests that autistic people tend to focus on the details unless they are asked to consider the bigger picture, in which case they can do so.

Self-advocacy and neurodiversity

Initially the discussion about autism took place mainly among professionals and parents, and autism was described in terms decided on by onlookers rather than by the autistic people themselves. As we can see when we read the language used in the diagnostic criteria described above, autism was spoken about using language that always identified it as a problem – words such as 'impairment', 'disorder', 'dysfunction'.

The adoption of a spectrum model for autism diagnosis and the recognition of Asperger syndrome led to many people being diagnosed with autism who were very intelligent, articulate and able to describe their experiences and advocate for themselves. As these autistic people came to terms with their diagnoses it was against a backdrop of the wider struggle for the recognition and rights of disabled people. Society was made aware of how an understanding of diversity and a willingness to make simple accommodations would allow disabled people to contribute to their communities and have the opportunity to reach their potential.

As autistic voices began to be heard they caused attitudes towards autism to change. Rather than seeing their autism as a bundle of deficits, which science should try to cure, the emerging autistic community began to identify the strengths that autism gave them. Perspectives began to be flipped over. An inability to see the bigger picture became a heightened ability to process details; a preoccupation with a special interest previously dismissed as obsessive became recognised as passion and expertise.

Although autistic people may find it harder to generalise, they are often strong when it comes to understanding or creating systems. One theory of autism, the empathising/systemising theory, sees the repetitive behaviour presented by autistic people in terms of an intelligent behaviour (a drive to systemise) rather than in terms of impairment in other areas.[6]

At the same time, technology began to change the way in which we all communicate. The development of the internet made it much easier for communities to develop around a common interest and this way of communicating is often far better suited to autistic people. Autistic communities began to develop in which autistic people themselves called the shots and defined the way in which they wanted to be seen and were able to tell the world what they needed.

Autistic people can now begin to assert themselves more than ever before and ensure that they are heard. There are many books and blogs in which a wide range of autistic people describe their personal experiences or talk about autism in general and educate the wider population. The input of these voices is invaluable to society in coming to terms with how best to ensure that autistic people get the chance to fulfil their potential.

From the autistic community comes the concept of neurodiversity. Neurodiversity describes the fact that all of our brains function in different ways and it would be wrong to assume that one way is superior to all others. Autistic people set standards of excellence in many different fields. It should be recognised that this is often because of somebody's autism, rather than despite it, and autism should be valued accordingly.

There is still some controversy about whether the autistic community can claim to speak for all autistic people. Parents of children whose autism causes them profound impairment may disagree with some of the assertions made by members of the autistic community, who may be successful people with Asperger syndrome, when they claim to be able to advocate for that parent's profoundly affected children.

As well as suggesting that you read further to increase your understanding of theory, I strongly recommend that you read some of the accounts written by autistic people themselves, both in print and online, if you wish to develop an insight into autism. The section of this chapter on executive function is drawn from the blog 'Musings of an Aspie', written by Cynthia Kim, and is a good place to start further reading.[7]

Throughout this book, I use the term 'autistic people' to describe people who have a diagnosis of autism spectrum disorder (ASD). I use this term because that is the way that autistic people themselves have told me they prefer to be addressed when autistic people are talked about in a general sense, as opposed to 'people with autism', which is often used by professionals.[8] Personally, I prefer the term ASC (autism spectrum condition) to ASD but use ASD in the text as this remains the official term for diagnosis. Apologies to any readers who prefer other terms to be used.

Why do neurotypical people lack empathy?

It is sometimes said that autistic people lack empathy. This assumption is increasingly being challenged. Empathy can be broken down into two components:

- Cognitive empathy: the ability to read someone else's feelings.

- Affective empathy: the tendency to respond emotionally (to care about and share) someone else's feelings.

Autistic people may find it difficult to read someone's feelings and see their perspective but they usually care a great deal as soon as they do pick up on those feelings, sometimes to the point of being overwhelmed.

From the perspective of an autistic person, many neurotypical people lack cognitive empathy. Most autistic people have found themselves in situations where neurotypical people have placed demands on them which no person with any capacity at all to understand their feelings would impose on them. For some autistic people this is a daily occurrence. Then they'll be told by those same neurotypical people that 'autistic people lack empathy'.

It is more accurate to talk about the 'double empathy problem', meaning that people whose cognitive functions are different often find it hard to have empathy for one another.

Changes to diagnosis and misdiagnosis

We have seen that the criteria for diagnosis have changed several times over the years. Although people who received a diagnosis based on the criteria laid out in *DSM-IV* will all retain their diagnosis, some of them would not be diagnosed as being autistic if they were to have waited until after *DSM-5* came out before they presented themselves to their physicians. They will, however, be presenting exactly the same behaviours and traits whatever the date may be.

Over the course of my career, I have also met several young people who have had an ASD diagnosis which has gone on to be questioned and then removed when they have been referred to a different specialist.

What does this mean from the point of view of someone providing Forest School?

It is important to understand that some other conditions can present in similar ways to autism and also that autistic traits are present in a great number of people at a level which is below the threshold for a clinical diagnosis. Lots of people are stronger systemisers than generalisers. People may have sensory processing issues but no other autistic traits, or may meet the criteria for social (pragmatic) communication disorder but not for ASD.

When working with children or young people you may find you have a learner identified by others as being 'probably autistic'. Some of these kids may go on to get a diagnosis, but many will not.

You should always put the person at the centre of your practice. Work with what you see. Starting out with a learner, you may initially need to rely on information given by others, but as you build your relationship with that learner consider what *they* are telling you, whether directly or through observation.

Some of the approaches described in this book will be relevant to that learner whether or not they are ever diagnosed under whatever the current diagnostic criteria are. I hope you will find this a useful resource but please always remember to be positive, not only in regard to autism in general, but in the value you place on all of the individuals who attend your sessions.

KEY POINTS

▶ Autism is a spectrum condition. A very broad range of people are diagnosed as being autistic. Although people will present a level of impairment in their social abilities and will present restricted and repetitive behaviours, the level of impairment varies a great deal between individuals.

▶ Many (although not all) autistic people also experience differences in sensory processing to a level which affects their day-to-day lives.

▶ Autistic people perceive the world in ways that are different from typical thinkers but these differences can be strengths as well as weaknesses.

▶ The criteria for an ASD diagnosis has changed at regular intervals. Autistic traits that fall below the threshold for diagnosis are common in the general population.

▶ In order to offer autism-inclusive practice, you must view each autistic person as an individual.

CHAPTER 3

The Benefits of Forest School

Before beginning to discuss the benefits that Forest School can bring to autistic people it is important that we pause and take a deep breath. The history of autism is littered with fads, cons and quackery that have been sold to autistic people and their families, often in good faith, but sometimes for purely exploitative reasons. While Forest School can bring positive benefits to autistic people, the degree to which it does so depends on the individual involved and what their needs and preferences are. It isn't a magic bullet. Autistic people do not all possess an innate affinity with nature and although some of my learners visibly calm as soon as they walk into woodland and seem more at ease sitting by a campfire among the trees than they do elsewhere, others have come to sessions and not been able to bear the feel of rain on their skin, preferring instead to be at home playing on an Xbox!

Although there is a growing evidence base[1] to show the benefits of increased contact with the natural world for people in general, there is not currently a strong evidence base to indicate any benefits of outdoor education specific to autistic learners and at the time of writing this area is under-researched.[2]

So, with our disclaimer firmly in place, we can begin to consider what Forest School can bring to autistic learners.

When discussing 'autistic learners' it should be clear that we are describing a very disparate group of people ranging from those with very high levels of intelligence and ability to others who present as having profound learning disabilities. Add to this that in the context of Forest School we may be talking about people of all ages from toddlers to the elderly (the oldest learner in my sessions is in his late 60s). The types of groups that people attend may be mainstream groups made up of mainly neurotypical learners, autism-specific groups or learning disability groups where people present various complex conditions. These groups may be accessed as part of a nursery, school or day-care provision or people may choose to attend Forest School as a standalone activity. What benefits can we offer autistic learners?

Creating inclusive spaces

I really enjoyed my Forest School training and learned a lot. Perhaps the most important lesson came on the first day. The class was taken into the forest to try out some practical activities. It was autumn and the woods were full of the beautiful range of colours that nature presents to us in that season. I was very excited and looking forward to taking part in practical activities and eagerly listened to our instructor as he set out our first task. We were asked to collect the colours of the rainbow from things that we could find in the forest, arrange them and then sing 'I Can See a Rainbow'. My heart sank. I am pretty much tone deaf and my singing voice is best described as the noise one might hear if a disgruntled badger were to argue with a goose. This wasn't my main concern though. I am colour blind and find it hard to distinguish between red and green at a certain point in the spectrum. As I walked through the woods looking for objects I was desperately trying to work out if the autumnal leaves were green or red and my inability to carry out the exercise filled me with a sense of failure.

This activity made me aware of a disability that does not usually have any effect on my day-to-day life. Forest School had made me disabled! It was a valuable lesson on the importance of being aware of learners' needs in order to ensure that any challenges are achievable and that our practice is inclusive.

When a Forest School group walks into the woods they are going on a journey into a different environment. A Forest School practitioner has the opportunity to make this into an inclusive space for everyone in their group and to demonstrate the importance of people valuing one another. Subsequent chapters will cover some of the practical approaches that we can take in order to achieve this with autistic participants.

By developing an awareness of the needs of our different learners we can plan activities that will engage them and give them the opportunity to learn and to achieve. When this is done sensitively, we can accommodate individual needs in a way that diminishes the impact of perceived disabilities and allows the person's strengths to shine through. However, if we don't take the time to try to understand and meet their needs we can have the opposite effect. It is not difficult to accommodate the different needs and preferences of individuals into sessions, and with a little forethought and preparation, everyone can benefit. Mixed groups can learn to value difference and the importance of including everybody in our communities.

A holistic approach

Forest School should not be viewed as an isolated activity but as a holistic part of someone's education or support. The insights provided by Forest School observations can bring great benefit when shared with others involved with the support or education of the autistic person and, particularly in the case of people with Asperger syndrome, can encourage reflection and development in the learner themselves. We should always be aiming for Forest School to follow a holistic approach and to work in partnership with the participant and any supporters in order to achieve best outcomes. Sessions are planned to work alongside the school curriculum or any individual development programme.

CASE STUDY:
Applying observations to support plans

O is a young man who is diagnosed as having ASD with moderate learning disability. He is literate and shows some understanding of numeracy. He recognises numbers, can tell the time and uses digital scales independently, showing a clear understanding of amounts to add or take away to measure the weight set out in a recipe. However, he has always struggled to grasp the value of money when shopping, which has hindered his independence in this area.

In Forest School sessions, he was observed to present indications of a predominately kinaesthetic learning style and displayed a high level of skill in working with his hands. If activities did not involve manual tasks, he would create his own by picking up sticks to break, moving branches or rocks and so on. He showed a noticeably lower level of engagement in tasks that were predominately visual.

The group created a 'Forest School Shop'; they cut small rounds of ash wood to use as 'coins' of different values and exchanged these for different snacks at tea break. O showed a good understanding of token exchange, including the concept that different tokens had different values and could 'buy' different types of biscuits, which also had different values.

O's team had been trying to teach him money recognition using photocopied sheets depicting different combinations of coins. By identifying a preference for kinaesthetic learning we were able to suggest O would have a better chance of learning if there was a kinaesthetic element to his money-handling lessons, rather than the purely visual one his team were using, and he actually got to hold and move around real money during the exercise.

This holistic approach includes any staff or carers who attend with the learners. Staff or carers are often outside their comfort zone when they first come into the woods with the group. They are learning new skills and routines together with the people they're supporting and this encourages them to see the learners from a new perspective.

Autistic people's difficulties with communication combined with the 'double empathy problem' can lead to assumptions being made by staff about the people they are teaching or supporting. Assumptions can also be based on staff generalising in a way in which the autistic person does not. Staff approaches can become quite rigid and inflexible and they often become more bound by routine than the people they are supporting. In some cases, these assumptions can be passed down through support teams for years. They may lead to people not being offered choices or opportunities as it has been assumed that they will not be interested – sometimes based on events from long ago and on a staff misunderstanding at the time.

The fresh perspectives that support staff gain when they first come to Forest School are valuable because they are experiential. The man who 'doesn't like to get his hands dirty' is happily collecting firewood, making dough or modelling with clay. The boy who 'only seems settled when he is sat looking at a screen' is calmly fuelling the fire. Assumptions are challenged most effectively by direct experience and when this happens, new opportunities can be opened up for the learner in other areas of their life.

At the time of writing social care in the UK is undergoing a period of crisis. Years of cuts to budgets are taking their toll on services. Staff turnover is high and morale is low. Staff may be inexperienced and Forest School is a valuable opportunity to model and encourage best practice. The learner-led approach of Forest School closely mirrors the person-centred approaches of social care and this has a great deal to offer to staff as well as learners.

Staff who attend my sessions not only get an opportunity to improve their practice and their understanding of the people they teach or support but they also get to have fun. When the time came for the staff from one of my sessions to choose a team-building activity they all asked to come to the woods have their own Forest School session without the people they support. We should never underestimate the importance for a person receiving support of having happy, positive supporters, and we can help to encourage this in Forest School sessions.

The holistic approach is not just about working in partnership with the learner themselves and their support or teaching staff who attend alongside them. Other professionals can have valuable input into planning sessions for a learner, and occupational therapists and speech and language therapists come to my sessions to make sensory observations and to observe participants' communication. This feedback is incorporated into our approach with learners and into an individual's development targets.

Health

I was one of those kids who was always running off to make camps in the woods. I loved it so much that I grew up to be the type of adult who lives in a camp in the woods. I like being out in nature and the outdoor life brings many benefits. Practical outdoor activities make us fit and are a great way to encourage exercise in those who would rather give a gym a wide berth or view PE lessons with a mixture of horror and disdain (I am guilty on both counts).

Research shows that autistic people have differences in the way they regulate the stress hormone cortisol and that exercise is effective in helping to counteract this imbalance. This can be a very important element in helping autistic people to manage the higher levels of stress and anxiety which cause significant challenges in their day-to-day lives.[3]

Forest School involves walking, carrying kit, collecting wood for fires or to build dens with, sawing, building and other forms of exercise. My favoured type of exercise is to keep fit by stealth, meaning you're so caught up in the activity that you don't realise that it's exercise at the time!

I had an autistic colleague who worked with me who refused any attempts by his support to encourage him to visit the gym, or even walk to the shops, but would carry kit across fields to our site in the woods. The track out of the woods is quite steep and this man found it quite a challenge, going so far as describing it as his 'nemesis', but despite this he would come every week and determinedly march up that track with a heavy bag of kit on his back.

One of the attractions of working in both support work and Forest School is the chance to witness those moments when an individual shines. Support work can be a thankless task. You work long hours for low pay and it is an increasingly low-status job. However, on some shifts you witness things that make it all worthwhile. I've been lucky to see lots of instances of this but one that sticks in my mind happened in Brighton near the beginning of my career. I was working a late shift and was scheduled to support a young man to visit a karaoke evening in a local bar. We took the bus together into town and when we walked into the pub it was already busy. As we made our way to the bar to order a drink the man I was with showed his excitement by 'stimming' – putting his arms up, elbows bent and palms open at head height and rocking his body backward and forward. His dress sense was more conservative than most people of his age and this, together with the stimming, was drawing the glances which some people cannot help but give when they don't understand the behaviour they are seeing. He ordered a soft drink at the bar and his tone and rhythm of speech, together with the formal language he used, further marked out his difference from the other drinkers. We sat and watched a couple of people sing and then it was time for the man I was with to step forward and take his turn. He announced the song he was going to sing in the same clipped and formal way in which he had ordered his drink and the crowd looked at him, seeing his perceived disability above all else. Then he began to sing. His voice was clear, strong and pitch perfect. His timing and phrasing were beautiful. His voice soared above the crowd, and in that moment they stopped seeing the disabled man. They saw the man with the beautiful voice. The best singer of the whole evening.

A central tenet of Forest School is raising learner's self-esteem through achievable challenges. The difficulties caused by a lack of autism awareness in wider society can often impact negatively on an individual's feelings of self-worth. This particularly applies if the person has Asperger syndrome and is very self-aware, and can lead to mental health problems and isolation if it is not addressed. Research has shown that 84.1 per cent of autistic people suffer from an anxiety disorder[4] and 1 in 15 people with Asperger syndrome suffer from depression.[5] By presenting people with an inclusive, autism-aware environment in which they have the opportunity to achieve we can raise their self-esteem, improve their well-being and empower them to realise their potential.

We all need to be given the opportunity to succeed and part of the satisfaction of providing Forest School is the chance to create these opportunities for people. One of my favourite moments in my early Forest School sessions was doing leaf rubbing with a man, P. P did not have very good fine motor skills so I held the clipboard, paper and leaf while he scribbled with the crayon. As the intricate outline of the leaf appeared on the paper, P was overjoyed and began to call to the other support worker, 'Look! Look what I've done!' He was praised by staff and his sense of achievement was clear to all. He took his leaf rubbing back to show to others after the session.

Providing these positive experiences increases the self-esteem and confidence of learners, leading to increased personal well-being, and also raises the esteem in which an individual is held by peers and supporters. Recognising an individual's achievements and valuing them increases the respect which they are shown by others and helps to build the inclusive spaces we are aspiring to create in our sessions.

Learning new skills and reinforcing existing ones

Forest School is a great place to learn new skills and to reinforce existing ones. The learner-led approach of Forest School encourages self-advocacy and promotes choice making and independence. This approach encourages learners' individual needs to be assessed based on observations and for sessions to be planned taking these needs into account.

New skills may include green woodwork, tree and nature identification, craft skills, fire starting or bushcraft, but Forest School is not just limited to the type of things that first spring into people's minds when they think of woodland activities. The only limits to what can be included in a session are the needs of the learners and the creativity of the Forest School practitioner!

Forest School is a great place to practise existing skills and can encourage an autistic learner to transfer skills into a different setting. When people use existing skills, observations can be made of how easy an individual finds it to generalise skills that they have learned elsewhere into a new situation. A good example of this is cooking skills for adult learners. You will be amazed at what you can cook on a campfire! My crowning glory so far has been cooking Christmas dinner with a group (although we did buy a pre-cooked turkey to avoid the risk of giving people food poisoning for Christmas!). As well as practising food preparation skills, some people who are reluctant to try new foods in other settings have shown an increased willingness to try new tastes when we have cooked them outdoors.

Sessions can be planned to incorporate a person's strengths and interests. Learners who display strengths in systemising may enjoy the challenge of building physical structures such as dens or hazel furniture (almost like outdoor Minecraft!). Others may show an ability to visually recognise and categorise trees and plants or an interest in discussing scientific processes such as charcoal making.

Those with learning disabilities will all have areas in which they show strengths, and activities can be broken down into separate tasks to ensure that everyone has a role in which they can achieve. People's interests can be incorporated into tasks – one of the learners in my sessions built a train outline from twigs, with smoke made from string curling out of its funnel, and then built a track from sticks which wound between the trees and around our camp.

Sometimes we may be lucky enough to notice a particular talent which a learner possesses and be able to encourage its development.

CASE STUDY:
Encouraging talents

T is a young man with a diagnosis of ASD and learning disabilities. He attends Forest School sessions and takes part well in many activities but tends to try to avoid fine motor tasks, although he has been observed to be able to carry them out competently. He seeks visual stimuli above others in the woods and will lie looking up at the patterns of light coming through the branches above him or sit watching flames quietly and contentedly. I often give learners a chance to use my evidence camera to take photos if they are not interested in the activity we are carrying out. When T was given the camera, he was very focused on taking pictures, moving around the site and selecting scenes to photograph. Later when I looked through the photos which he had taken I was struck by how good they were. T's visual abilities led him to take pictures with a good sense of composition. His interest in photography is now encouraged by his team and he uses his own camera and selects his favourite pictures on the computer back at his flat.

Sensory benefits

In Chapter 2 we described the differences in sensory processing that many autistic people experience. People spend much of their lives in manmade indoor spaces but Forest School takes place outdoors. Natural settings tend to be very rich in the range of sensory stimuli presented, but these stimuli are usually less intense than those found in manmade environments. For example, natural light under a forest canopy is far gentler than the strip lights found in many conventional classrooms, and the objects which light falls on are seldom reflective in the way that many surfaces indoors may be.

We will discuss the sensory elements of Forest School in Chapter 7, but this aspect of sessions can be very beneficial to learners.

An individual's sensory needs can be met very well by the combination of a learner-led approach and an outdoor environment. As long as some basic safety procedures are followed, Forest School provides an opportunity to satisfy an individual's needs to engage with, or avoid, different stimuli. All of the senses can be used at Forest School and this is particularly useful if people have to spend time in other spaces, such as classrooms, where this may not always be possible.

Stimuli that are needed can be offered in an inclusive way; for instance, a child in a mixed group can be offered the vestibular stimuli of a rope swing, hammock or mud slide if they require this, and this can be shared with their neurotypical classmates in a fun way. In a classroom, where they may be expected to sit still, efforts by the child to create these stimuli could exclude them from their peers. By sharing the activity and having fun together the child's classmates can see what they get from vestibular stimuli and be encouraged to understand one another's needs.

Some people who present sensory processing differences are encouraged to follow a 'sensory diet'. Sensory diets are created with occupational therapists to meet an individual's sensory needs. They offer the person the sensory stimuli they need, to a level which satisfies them, and are found to help an individual to concentrate, to lessen anxiety and to improve communication, motor skills and learning.[6] The sensory environment of Forest School can give the individual the opportunity to experience the stimuli they need as part of their sensory diet and this can be incorporated into activities in a fun way.

As well as the benefits of autistic learners meeting their immediate sensory needs during the session, our observations of learners can provide very useful insights when applied holistically. An awareness of the impact that differences in sensory processing can have on a person, and an understanding of how to lessen this impact, is often a central part of helping someone to reach their potential. Sensory sensitivity, whether hyper (over) or hypo (under), can make it difficult to focus attention and can trigger anxiety or exacerbate stress that someone is already experiencing. Observations of sensory interaction at Forest School can help to build a 'sensory profile' of a person's individual sensory preferences and how they may fluctuate. This information can be used by the person themselves, and their supporters, to work out calming strategies or to make accommodations that will help them to feel more comfortable and to focus better.

Social interaction

Social interaction is an important part of Forest School. Participants communicate, cooperate and, it is hoped, have fun together. Neurotypical learners often show improvements in communication, problem solving and conflict resolution after attending Forest School.[7]

The social aspect of Forest School is equally important for autistic people. In Chapter 2 we looked at the ways that autism causes impairments in social communication and imagination but it is important to understand that this does not mean that autistic people do not enjoy being in the company of others or place value on their relationships. Almost every autistic person I have met has clearly shown that relationships with significant people are important to them. Even people who present profound impairments in communication and learning disabilities will respond with unmistakable pleasure when they see members of their family, friends or favoured members of staff if they have not seen them for some time.

The nature of autism is such that people may have trouble expressing how they feel and interacting in a way that neurotypicals naturally understand and this can be made worse by clumsy attempts to make the autistic person conform to neurotypical expectations.

Forest School has the potential to create inclusive opportunities for the learner to cooperate in group tasks, share sensory experiences and promote an understanding of how to value difference. Social connections can be made in an experiential learning environment that do not have to rely on the areas of social communication in which the learner may be impaired. Sitting quietly around a fire, sharing food or all enjoying a hot drink can give a feeling of togetherness to people which does not require talking or an awareness of people's tone of voice or body language. A clear role in a differentiated group task can give someone the satisfaction of cooperating with others to achieve a goal as a valued part of a team.

Activities can provide a chance to develop or reinforce social skills such as patience, sharing or turn taking, and the use of communication systems or interventions should be continued at Forest School to ensure that sessions link holistically with the rest of a learner's support or education.

Our Forest School sessions can be an important tool in helping someone reach their potential if we take the time to understand and value difference.

Forest School as a career

Autistic people set standards of excellence in pretty much every field of human endeavour. There is no reason that Forest School should be any different. I once worked with autistic colleagues to provide sessions and create a voluntary work placement for a young autistic man. The man who worked alongside me as a volunteer attended the 2015 Laing Buisson Awards to represent our team when we were selected as finalists in the Autism Category, and he went on to be awarded the runner up in The National Autistic Society Volunteer of the Year:

> It was a great learning experience. Seeing people with autism in a natural outdoor environment was interesting. It was a lot of fun and I was interested in seeing autism from a different perspective. It's helped me to learn some of the organisational life skills I'll need to move on into other employment. (JB, volunteer staff)

Having read through the potential benefits which Forest School can offer to autistic people you will probably have noticed that many of them are shared with any other type of learner. What struck me when I started to run Forest School sessions were the similarities between autistic people and neurotypicals. In my career as a support worker, the focus was often on the differences and, in particular, the impairments which people presented but delivering Forest School has made me primarily aware of the participants' strengths and of the things which we have in common. I feel that this perspective increases the understanding of neurodiversity and reinforces the importance of inclusivity.

I've left the greatest benefit of Forest School until last. It's the simplest but it is by far the most important. It should underpin practice in every session. Forest School is fun. Having fun together breaks down barriers. It makes learning and development a pleasure rather than a chore. It relieves stress and promotes well-being. Every day I go to work I have fun. I love the company of my learners. We smile and laugh, share food and drinks and we're playful. Autistic people may sometimes play in a different way to others, but once you've worked out how to join in you're going to have a great time.

KEY POINTS

▶ Forest School offers a range of benefits to participants. There is a growing body of research that evidences positive outcomes among neurotypical participants, but there is a lack of research into benefits specific to autistic learners.

▶ Forest School follows a learner-led approach and this flexibility makes it easier to achieve autism-inclusive practice.

▶ Forest School's individualised approach should tie in with any educational curriculum or personal development plan that a participant is working towards. This holistic approach encourages personal progression.

▶ The holistic approach includes the learner's supporters, encourages a better understanding of the learner and aims to promote best practice among supporters.

▶ Benefits to health are both physical, through exercise and promoting healthy choices, and emotional, through boosting self-esteem.

▶ Activities can reinforce existing skills and teach new ones. Learning opportunities are person centred and are in no way restricted to bushcraft or nature activities. Sessions can incorporate a learner's special interests and the learner-led approach is flexible in meeting individual needs.

▶ Autistic people often have sensory processing differences. These differences can make the sensory environment a very important consideration. Natural sensory environments, combined with the flexibility of a learner-led approach, have the potential to meet autistic people's sensory needs.

▶ The individualised approach of Forest School can provide inclusive social opportunities by respecting participants' differences and allowing them to interact with others on their own terms.

- ▶ People can be supported to develop social skills and strategies in an inclusive environment.

- ▶ Autistic people can also participate in Forest School as Forest School leaders, assistants or volunteers.

- ▶ Most importantly of all, Forest School is great fun!

CHAPTER 4

Preparation! Preparation! Preparation!

The key to providing inclusive Forest School sessions is preparation – preparation before a course of sessions begins and ongoing reflection, consideration and preparation once they are under way.

In Chapter 2, we discussed the individual nature of autism which lies behind the generalisations used in diagnostic criteria. To meet the needs of the people attending your session you must begin by viewing all of your learners as individuals. You need to understand that you are also a learner, getting to know the people attending your session and learning how to best meet their needs.

The famous author and autism spokesperson Temple Grandin used the memorable phrase 'An anthropologist on Mars' to describe how she felt in typical social situations, and one of the leading autistic online communities is called 'Wrong Planet'.[1] From the perspective of a neurotypical person who interacts a lot with autistic people, I don't feel that I am dealing with people from another planet. For all our differences, I feel that we share a lot more common ground than that. However, every time I meet a new autistic person it can feel as though I'm going on a journey to a different country. I have to begin to learn a new language in order to communicate, and new customs and etiquette in order to avoid giving offence.

Inclusive practice

Inclusion is the practice of making sure that everyone, regardless of any perceived differences, is valued and can take part in society.

Inclusion is not simply a matter of ensuring that everyone who wants to can access your session. It is not about people simply being present, but about them being involved and feeling valued.

Are there meaningful activities that everyone can be involved in? This does not mean denying one member of your group an opportunity because another may not be able to take part in it. If there is an activity which some members of your group can benefit from but some will struggle to achieve, then you should offer a choice of activities, each being equally attractive to learners.

As an example, cast your mind back to the part of the last chapter where I described myself disconsolately searching for different coloured leaves during my training. Colour blind in the cold November rain. Did I mention it was raining? It was. Absolutely pouring down. This activity could have been made more inclusive by offering choices. Rather than being given only one task – finding colours then singing about them (which other members of the group enjoyed) – we could have been offered a choice between that and searching for interesting shapes and then telling a story about them. I could have chosen to follow a task I could do and which my disability did not prevent me from achieving.

In order to know which choices would have been relevant in the above situation the practitioner would have needed to be informed beforehand of my colour blindness.

When we consider the needs of our group we need to be aware of individual differences, in order to make accommodations that will lessen their impact, but we should not allow this to become our main focus. Don't become trapped in asking, 'What can't they do?' Instead start by asking, 'What can they do?'

Consider my example again. I'm colour blind. I just can't distinguish certain colours. It's not something I can learn. However, I can see shapes and I love telling a story. Offer me a choice I can take part in and give me the chance to achieve.

Many of the activities that take place during Forest School sessions can be broken down into steps. Some learners may not be able to carry out all of the steps but will be able to achieve parts of the task. In this case, you can allocate roles for carrying out certain steps and working as a team. Each member of the team is important because without them their step in the process wouldn't happen. For example, let's break down having a fire:

- Someone needs to collect and carry wood back to camp.

- Someone needs to ensure that the fire pit area is clear of brash and trip hazards.

- Someone needs to make sure there is a bucket of water to hand. They may need to collect water from the nearest water source.

- Someone needs to process the wood – sawing, snapping up or sorting the wood into different sizes.

- Someone needs to build and light the fire.

- When the fire is lit, someone needs to make sure everyone is following safety rules.

- Someone needs to fuel the fire.

- Someone needs to put the fire out completely once we're done.

All of the people who attend my sessions can carry out at least one of the steps and make up a valued part of the fire-lighting team.

Inclusion does not mean wrapping a person up in cotton wool and stopping them from facing challenges. A central part of the Forest School ethos is building self-esteem through facing and overcoming achievable challenges. This applies to all members of the group. An awareness of an individual's needs should take into account the difference between not being able to do something at all and finding something difficult. People with a perceived disability need to build self-confidence and resilience at least as much as those who are not considered disabled. When planning activities, ensure that they contain achievable challenges for all participants.

Inclusive Forest School sessions should provide an environment where everyone taking part has their needs accommodated, feels valued and is involved, on their own terms, in enjoyable activities that will challenge and promote growth and development.

What do we need to know when we prepare our sessions to make this relevant to autistic people? Let's consider who needs to know what and when they need to consider it. That breaks down to:

Who?

- The Forest School practitioner and their team.

- The individual learners and their supporters (which may include teachers, families and support staff).

When?

- Before a course of sessions begins.

- During the course of sessions – based on feedback from the group, observations and reflection and assessment.

Preparation before a course of sessions begin

Initial preparation is very important when seeking to include autistic learners. New situations can be very stressful for autistic people and one of the keys to alleviating this is to ensure that steps have been taken to prepare the autistic person, and their support, for what Forest School is going to involve and what they can expect to happen. The autistic person will need to let the Forest School practitioner know of any additional needs they have so that these can be thought about in advance and any necessary accommodations can be put in place from the outset.

What's the system?

In my own practice, I have found it very useful whenever I meet a new learner to begin by asking myself, 'What's the system?'

In Chapter 2 we mentioned the 'empathising/systemising theory' and the tendency to show strength in creating, recognising and using systems, which many autistic people present. What do we mean by this?

Systemising describes the tendency to understand, and create, systems. A system is something which consistently follows set rules. Examples of systems include:

- mechanical systems such as engines or the doors of a cabinet

- abstract systems such as mathematical equations or computer coding

- natural systems such as seasons or the weather

- collectible systems such as alphabetised record collections or arranging favourite objects in a consistent pattern.

People with a diagnosis of ASD have been found to show particular strength in systemising. Even the repetitive behaviour of people who are diagnosed as having significant learning disabilities often display a strong urge to create consistent systems.

As a Forest School practitioner, I seek to develop a trusting relationship with the learners who attend my sessions. An awareness of an autistic learner's systems is an important foundation for building that trust.

Different systems have different functions. Some autistic people develop their own systems to help them overcome problems that their autism is causing them. These systems can take many forms and may be simple, or very complex. When people are verbally communicating by using a narrow repertoire of repetitive phrases, we may be seeing a communication system that reflects how that person processes communication and one that the person has naturally developed in order to overcome difficulty in interacting with others (this will be discussed in the next chapter). Some people develop repetitive physical systems of movement, which help them to calm when they are feeling stressed. I recently heard about an autistic boy who has created a complex system based on Minecraft which he uses to process and understand social situations. Some systems have been created by others. Daily schedules are systems that may have been created by the person using them, but which often have had the input of supporters. Autistic people often show great interest in systems such as bus timetables or rail networks.

Autistic people's use of systems is often described in negative terms due to the inflexibility they can present when using them. *DSM-IV* criteria describes routines which the individual may be very focused on as being non-functional. Personally, I do not see an autistic person's routines or rituals as non-functional at all. Their routines and rituals may not be immediately clear to a neurotypical person but they have a clear function to the person who uses them and they are important to that person, and if you are trying to adopt an empathetic approach then you should not take a dismissive attitude towards them. I would suggest that you view this trait in positive terms. Pretty much everyone uses systems of some type and this is one area where neurotypicals should be able to find some common ground with autistic people. When preparing to include an autistic person in your sessions, find out which of the systems that they use are relevant to their time at your session. The more you learn about their systems, the better your relationship with them will be.

As well as being aware of their systems, ensure that the sessions have systems in place that the autistic person can identify with and learn from. If you are already delivering Forest School then think about your sessions from the point of view of systems. You probably already have lots of systems in place. Do your sessions have a structure? Do they start at a set time and in a set place? Do you begin walking to a set area, then briefing the group? Is there a regular time to stop for a drink and snack? To clear up and finish the session? That's a system.

Structure is important to autistic learners. A consistent structure provides a level of predictability which helps to reduce stress and helps the person feel grounded. In Chapter 2, we discussed how autistic ways of thinking can make it hard to shift attention, to initiate actions and to sequence options. Autistic people can find it difficult when they transition between activities. The function of a consistent structure is to accommodate these ways of thinking. People can learn to recognise the point when it is time to move on to the next part of the sequence in your session, which will help them to make the transition between your activities. Structure is also important if a person feels overwhelmed and stressed, as it can be easier to calm if there is a predictable structure to return to.

When teaching new skills to your autistic learner it can help to break the process down. Create steps and follow them in a consistent order every time you carry out the task. As an example, let's think about safely using a bowsaw. As you consider the steps, think about them as a physical system of movement as well as a safety routine:

- Take the safety gloves and bowsaw from the tool bag.

- Put a glove on one hand, leaving the hand which will hold the saw bare.

- Remove the safety guard from the bowsaw blade.

- Place the safety guard in a spot within reach but out of the way of the work you are about to do.

- As soon as you have finished sawing, replace the safety guard on the blade in the correct manner.

- Return the saw and glove to the tool bag.

Think about some of the things which you do in your sessions and break them down into steps (if you aren't currently running sessions then think about some of your day-to-day chores). Try to develop an awareness of everyday systems and use this to inform your approaches when working with autistic learners.

When observing a learner in the woods you will notice which steps they can carry out independently and which they need a little support with. You can praise the parts of the tasks they are achieving and focus in on the parts they are still learning, withdrawing support at the pace at which they pick up the skill. A consistent system which the autistic learner can recognise may make it easier for them to learn the new skill.

Some learners may have a predisposition to collect and categorise. The Forest School environment is full of opportunities to use this strength. Natural spaces are rich in a diverse variety of flora and fauna and some learners may like to engage with the woods by identifying different species, categorising them and learning about the systems of co-dependence which make up their local ecosystem.

When considering how to apply systems in your practice, beware the common pitfall of becoming inflexible and forgetting the point of the system in the first place. In my experience, it is common for people supporting an autistic person to become more bound by routine than the autistic person themselves. The routines we use change at different points throughout our lives when they no longer serve the function for which they were developed. Systems change as circumstances change. You are not programming automatons. Systems are only useful in so far as they are successful in helping the people using them.

In my experience, the level of 'inflexible rigidity' in following routines and rituals varies greatly from individual to individual and from one situation to another. If someone is feeling safe and calm and is given as much prior warning as possible, with effective communication, then they will often cope well with change. If change is sudden and there is a lack of effective communication, then you must expect people to become stressed.

Routines and rituals are not all of equal importance to the learner, and the practitioner needs to learn which are their priorities and when. Remember that autistic people will tend to be focused on the details of the system and you may tend to overlook these and see the bigger picture. You will need to become empathetic to the perspective of your autistic learner.

Sudden, unexpected changes to plan cause stress when they happen to neurotypical people but a neurotypical person can usually see the bigger picture and quickly resequence the plan in their head while their executive function inhibits their stress responses and initiates alternative action. The autistic person's responses will not be as effective in the same situation and they may feel disorientated and overwhelmed and be unable to control a sense of panic. The practitioner needs to reflect on how to avoid this situation developing. An awareness of the function of structure and systems and how the learner uses them will help you to develop empathy for the learner and to consider their needs.

Forest School practice is learner led. When using systems be led, as far as is possible, by the person attending the session. If you are reflecting on a system you have created then ask yourself if the system in question is one you can afford to change. Possibly not if it's a safety routine, but otherwise be prepared to be flexible if that is where your learner is leading. Work towards an empathetic understanding of the systems which the learner has brought with them and the levels of importance they attribute to them.

Questions to ask

Before beginning sessions, we should ask the people who are going to attend a few questions. There will be information you need that applies to every type of learner, such as health and dietary requirements, and some additional information that you should consider asking for from an autistic learner.

It is up to you how you get this information but I would recommend a brief questionnaire so that you have a permanent record of people's needs. I would suggest that the questions address the learner in the first person, to encourage their involvement in advocating for themselves, even if you are aware that someone else will be supporting them to complete the form.

People will only need to share information with you if it is appropriate for you to know it in order to accommodate their needs and ensure their safety. Any information about a person should be treated as being confidential and processed and stored according to your country's data protection laws.

Health issues

You will need to be made aware of any health issues participants may have if they could be an issue during sessions, for example asthma, diabetes, epilepsy, pica, allergies. Participants include any carers, support staff and teachers. We will discuss health issues in further depth in Chapter 8.

Dietary requirements

Choosing and preparing food and drink and sitting to share a meal or snack and reflect on the day is part of the structure of all of my sessions. It's good to know about people's dietary requirements to ensure that choices of food and drink offered in sessions are inclusive. Dietary requirements may reflect health needs, religious or cultural observance or personal preferences. Some autistic people can be very set in their food preferences and it is important that choices offered take into account all of the group's preferences so that no one is left out.

Accessibility/mobility issues

Does the learner have any issues with physical mobility? If so you must consider whether your site is accessible for them. Can you make it more accessible or would you need to use a different site? Find out if they have any physical issues that may affect their ability to take part in specific activities. Some autistic people may have impaired fine motor skills or movement and coordination problems. What accommodations can be made to overcome these issues? You may need to adapt equipment but often a little extra staff support is all that is required to help someone to take part. If the learner is not be able to take part in a specific activity then ensure that there is a choice of activities, *of equal appeal and value,* which can be offered to the whole group.

Preferred methods of communication

This is one of the key considerations when delivering Forest School to autistic people. Differences in communication are key criteria in the diagnosis of ASD. By the very nature of ASD, autistic learners will struggle to communicate on your terms so it is your responsibility to learn to communicate on theirs. We will discuss communication in greater depth in the following chapter, but what do we need to ask in our initial questions?

- How does the learner prefer to communicate? This may be verbally or using visual methods of communication, for example sign language, Picture Exchange Communication System (PECS) books or apps on tablets. In many of my groups, each learner may have a different individual method of communication, often combining several different communication systems.

- Does the learner use visual schedules or Social Stories™ and do they need you to provide any information or photographs to include in these?

- Are there any words or subjects that the learner does not like? Some autistic people have trigger words, phrases or topics of conversation that cause them to become stressed if they are spoken around them. These are sometimes associated with past experiences which were upsetting. Some examples of words that cause one of my learners to become stressed are 'haircut' and 'boat'. It's good to be forewarned if this applies to anyone in your group as it is very easy to avoid causing unnecessary stress by uttering the wrong word or phrase.

Sensory profile

As mentioned in Chapter 2, differences in sensory processing are a common feature of autism and can have a profound impact on a person's life. We will discuss the sensory aspects of Forest School in greater depth in Chapter 7, but what does the practitioner need to know before beginning a course of sessions?

- Does the learner have a sensory profile? This is a description of their sensory interactions – which stimuli they seek and which they avoid.

- Are they currently engaged with any sensory interventions, such as a sensory diet? If so, Forest School should aim to continue with these interventions during sessions and you should communicate with any occupational therapists or support staff who are implementing them and cooperate to make sure that Forest School is making a holistic contribution to these programmes.

At this stage, an awareness of a learner's sensory profile can be used to consider if any accommodations need to be made to reduce any irritation or stress that stimuli may cause them. Equally, you should begin to consider how to provide the stimuli that a learner seeks. This is often a key factor in engaging an autistic learner in Forest School.

Behavioural support

Does the learner have a plan in place for behavioural support? This will consist of agreed responses to specific behaviours the learner could present. It should identify triggers that cause stress, any signs which indicate that the learner is becoming stressed (sometimes described as coming off baseline) and agreed responses to help the learner to calm (return to baseline).

It's important that responses are consistent to support the learner to manage their behaviour when they are struggling to do this themselves. If a learner is attending with support it will be their responsibility to ensure that any plan is being followed, but even in this case you should be aware of what is expected of you.

Some learners may have developed their own coping strategies for dealing with stress and it would be useful if they could share these with you before sessions begin so that you can be clear about how they would like you to help. The learner will probably not be able to explain once they have become stressed and any spontaneous interventions you make by that point are likely to exacerbate the situation.

Likes and dislikes

Autistic people often have strong feelings about the things they like or dislike. We touched on 'special interests' in Chapter 2. These are a subject which a person is particularly focused on and they are very important to that person. Their pursuit brings positive benefits: pleasure, reducing anxiety, creating systems (such as categorising collections), providing a subject for conversation that the person feels in control of, or a sense of identity.

Sometimes people may have an interest that can be shared with others who share the enthusiasm, such as facts about sport or railways, but sometimes they may be considered eccentric by others, such as adult men who are very interested in My Little Pony® or a person who collects photographs of drain covers. Occasionally, people may require support to ensure that their interest does not affect their ability to carry out their day-to-day life and there may be strategies in place to support somebody to manage this.

Knowledge of a learner's special interests, and an empathetic approach to understanding their importance to that person, can be a key factor in beginning to build a trusting relationship with them. When you discover what someone's interest is you should prepare yourself to be open to their need to express it. Can the interest be included in their activities at Forest School? Be flexible and creative when you think about this. When planning sessions, think about any opportunities to include learners' special interests. If a learner wants to engage you in conversation about an interest which is not relevant to Forest School, take the time to be attentive but be prepared to set a boundary on how long you can discuss this with them. We will expand on this in the next chapter.

Some autistic people form an attachment to objects. Neurotypical people are hardwired to respond more to faces than objects, but functional magnetic resonance imaging (fMRI) scans of young adults with ASD have indicated that autistic people may have a propensity towards perceiving faces in the same way as objects.[2] Some of the learners who attend my sessions bring objects along which are very important to them. One man brings an old *Thomas the Tank Engine* book, which he carries and will hold up close to one of his eyes sometimes. Another man brings a postcard, which he likes to hold throughout the session. He changes these postcards for new ones at regular points in the day but I keep some spare ones in my emergency bag in case anything happens to his postcard during the session.

The best-known example of this is probably 'Jamie and the Lion'.[3] Jamie Knight is a successful website developer who carries a four-foot plush lion with him wherever he goes. Jamie explains that his Lion is a coping strategy which brings some consistency and control to his sensory environment. Jamie's Lion brings a consistent texture and smell, and hugging Lion gives Jamie proprioceptive stimulation, or deep pressure. Lion helps Jamie feel grounded if his environment is making him feel overloaded.

If a learner has an object they like to carry with them then ensure that they have the opportunity to bring it with them. Consider if it will affect their ability to take part in activities, and if any strategies are required if they have to put it down or give it to somebody to hold. Be aware that a person may need support if other members of the group interfere with the favourite object.

Autistic people can present an 'all or nothing' approach to things and be quite adamant in asserting this. This can sometimes manifest itself in phobias and you should be made aware if a learner has any phobias which could affect their experience of Forest School. It's best to think about how to accommodate phobias in advance and have a strategy worked out.

A common phobia for people I have supported over the years is dogs. The appearance of a dog can induce a very stressful reaction in some people. You need to be aware of this if your Forest School site is open to the public and used by dog walkers. Be aware of the paths dog walkers use and site your base camp off the path where you have a view of who is approaching. If you see a dog, then have a member of staff approach the dog owner and politely explain the situation. Ask if they would mind keeping the dog on a lead until they have passed the group. Try to ensure that the person who is afraid of dogs is away from the dog-walkers' route and try to keep them occupied with a distraction that is interesting to them (such as talking about a favourite subject, or doing a sensory activity). When choosing a site, you should consider how much it is used by dog walkers. The occasional dog walker is easy to manage but a steady, unpredictable stream of dogs would not be easy to manage if you have a learner who has this phobia.

Initial development targets: building a relationship

The Forest School practitioner should work with the individual learner and their supporters to establish how Forest School will contribute to any educational curriculum or development targets. This should be discussed before sessions begin, but the practitioner's initial focus should be to establish a relationship between themselves, the learner and the natural environment. This relationship is described by Sara Knight as 'a triangle of trust, respect and reliance'.[4] I believe that this approach, which lies at the heart of Forest School practice, is very well suited to working with autistic learners.

Hans Asperger described the attributes needed to teach the autistic students he had observed:

> These children often show a surprising sensitivity to the personality of the teacher. However difficult they are, even under optimal conditions, they can be guided and taught, but only by those who give them genuine affection, people who show kindness towards them and yes, humour. The teacher's underlying emotional attitude influences, involuntarily and unconsciously, the mood and behaviour of the child. Of course, the management and guidance of such children essentially requires a proper knowledge of their peculiarities as well as genuine pedagogic talent and efficiency.[5]

The Forest School approach requires the practitioner to build an empathetic, respectful relationship with each learner. The learner is accepted and valued on their own terms and is viewed as a partner in the experience. The practitioner seeks to make observations to provide individualised support to learners. This emphasis on trying to understand each learner on their own terms, and apply this understanding to contribute to their positive development, echoes the attributes that Asperger identified.

To succeed in establishing this relationship, the practitioner must learn to empathise with the autistic learner. This empathy is built on the twin foundations of general autism awareness and getting to know the learner as an individual.

Relationship with place

Forest School can lay no claim to having a monopoly on promoting an empathetic approach to learners – as we can see from the quote above, Asperger was describing this kind of approach long before Forest School began to come to widespread attention. What does differ is the importance that the Forest School approach places on the physical environment where sessions take place.

We have briefly mentioned the sensory differences experienced by many autistic people, and will discuss this in further detail later in the book. These differences in sensory perception can make the physical environment around an autistic person an important consideration. A heightened sense of place, experienced across different sensory domains, can make some environments very challenging. Conversely, some environments contain things that demand sensory exploration, which fascinate and absorb the person to the point that it is hard to focus attention elsewhere.

Environments designed to accommodate an autistic person's sensory needs are commonplace in settings created specifically for autistic people, whether in an individual's home or in community settings. Often though, these settings are autistic spaces. Public spaces that can meet all the needs of autistic people and neurotypicals simultaneously are, perhaps, less common. I feel that natural spaces, for many people, can provide inclusive sensory spaces and I will consider this in more depth in Chapter 7.

Autistic people not only experience a difference in the way that their senses process their physical surroundings but often connect with the physical world in preference to the social world.

Tony Attwood describes this tendency in early years children:

> Very young children with Asperger's syndrome in their preschool or kindergarten years may not be interested in the activities of their peers or making friends...are usually more interested in understanding the physical rather than the social world...to search for insects and reptiles, or gaze at cloud formations.[6]

He goes on to describe older children and adults:

> The person with Asperger's syndrome has a natural ability with the physical rather than the interpersonal world and this is reflected in the choice of interests (Baron-Cohen and Wheelwright 1999). While other children are exploring the social world, children with Asperger's syndrome are exploring objects, machines, animals and scientific concepts. We use the term 'the lifelong search for the pattern or meaning of life': those with Asperger's syndrome seem to have a natural ability to determine the function of objects, and an innate interest in what physically influences life, such as science (especially the weather and geography).[7]

We can see that Attwood is describing both the tendency to often be more interested in objects than other people, and the strengths in systemising, which we have also considered earlier in this chapter.

Attwood's quote regarding older children and adults is particularly interesting if considered alongside Richard Louv's description of 'the eighth intelligence' in *Last Child in the Woods*. Louv describes Professor Howard Gardner's theory of multiple intelligences.

Gardner was a professor of education at Harvard University who, in 1983, proposed that typical people present a broader range of intelligence than traditional IQ testing can measure. He originally proposed seven types of intelligence but went on to later add an eighth: naturalist intelligence. Professor Leslie Owen Wilson, an educational psychologist from the University of Wisconsin, went on to describe the profile of those who possess naturalist intelligence with the following characteristics:

1. Have heightened sensory awareness.

2. Use this sensory awareness to explore and understand the natural world.

3. Enjoy outdoor activities which involve engaging with nature.

4. Notice patterns in their surroundings.

5. Care about the natural world.

6. Notice details in nature which others might miss.

7. Record and curate records or collections which relate to their interests. For example, keep nature diaries, photo albums or collections of natural specimens.

8. Are interested from a young age in media which relates to nature.

9. Show an interest in conservation and environmental protection.

10. Find it easy to learn about and categorise data about the natural world.[8]

It's hard not to be struck by how much this description of 'the eighth intelligence' reads like the profile of a person with Asperger syndrome whose special interests involve nature.

I would argue that the combination of sensory processing differences and a tendency to naturally engage more with the physical environment than the social one can make the autistic person more present in the natural environment than the average neurotypical learner. However, I would caution against overstating, or romanticising, this and claiming that autistic people are all naturally tuned in to nature. In my experience, the object that the learner is most interested in is as likely to be the bowsaw as the tree. The zip on someone's anorak may be infinitely more fascinating than the sunlight falling through the leaf canopy!

However, I do feel that the Forest School approach is a pedagogy that has the potential to facilitate an autism-friendly learning environment more easily than many other approaches. Behaviours that seek to stimulate senses or try to interact with the physical environment are positively encouraged by the learner-led approach. A practitioner will set boundaries to ensure safety, and prevent harm to the environment, but beyond this there is a level of freedom to explore which has the potential to accommodate these behaviours. In fact, many Forest School activities seek to encourage neurotypical learners to engage their senses – sensory collecting, play in mud, rope swings, outdoor cooking – and to engage physically, using fine and gross motor skills by building dens, carrying firewood and using tools. These activities can be shared by both neurotypical and autistic learners and there is great potential to develop inclusive practice.

The Forest School approach places great emphasis on the connection between the people attending a session and the environment in which the session takes place. Place plays a key role in allowing learners the freedom to be physical, to use their bodies and their senses in the way in which they feel they need to. The amount of physical space to be found outdoors, particularly out in the woods, is a great boon for autistic learners. There is space to move – to rock, to jump or to sway – there is space to move away from anything you may not like, and there is space to be still. Different areas of the woods will hold different sensory stimuli and the learner is free to move into these spaces whenever they feel they need to. This awareness of the importance of encouraging learners to build their relationship with place can naturally facilitate an inclusive learning environment for autistic people.

As a practitioner, you should view gaining your own sense of place as an important part of your initial preparation. You should be aware of building your own relationship with your Forest School site.

I am lucky enough to live in woods where some of my sessions take place. We had been living here for years before I began to use the space for Forest School. We live off grid and have a close relationship with the natural environment. The woods behind us used to be a Victorian quarry and you can still see the walls of limestone standing at points throughout, but they are the only suggestion that industry ever happened here. There is a small patch of coniferous plantation but most of the trees in the wood are a mixture of sycamore, field maple and oak, with lines of hazel along boundaries where hedges once grew, overgrown now. Ash trees grow everywhere, with the young ash plants pushing up and taking over cleared areas. As I write this at the end of the winter, snowdrops have pushed through and catkins are beginning to show on the hazel. Soon patches of wood sorrel and bluebells will appear and ladies smock will grow again along the path.

There is a spring down in the woods which has only risen a couple of times this winter, water bubbling up from beneath the roots of an old ash tree and meandering down towards the bottom road in a stream. The woods are dominated by a huge badger sett which has been there for at least a hundred years, with smaller satellite setts all around. In the summer evenings you can see the badgers bustling along their runs, often with cubs in tow. Roe deer lie in the bracken along one bank, moving to bramble above where our Forest School base is if the weather has been very wet. In the spring, when they throw their usual caution to the wind, you will often see hares in the surrounding fields.

Rooks, pigeons and pheasants roost in the woods and every summer buzzards nest in the tall spruce trees above the spring, their young calling out across the wood. Woodpeckers are often heard, and sometimes seen, and as I lie in my bed I can hear the sounds of tawny owls and sometimes the screech of a barn owl, or vixens calling through the night to dog foxes.

Over the years, I have had the chance to observe how the woods change around me through the seasons. Fallen ash and hazel from the woods goes in the woodburner to keep us warm in the chill winter nights, wild garlic gets picked to be made into pesto (my children graze on it like little goats when they're out playing), sloes get picked off the blackthorn and steeped in gin to toast Christmas.

Despite this close relationship with the place where some of my sessions take place, I was taught new perspectives when I began to take learners into the woods. I became more aware of how the light falls in different spots by following my learners who were drawn to these places; they taught me to lie on my back and marvel at the way that light appears shining through the canopy above me, like the kaleidoscopes we looked through as children.

Most people do not have the opportunity to live in the place where their sessions occur but I would encourage practitioners to visit their sites outside their sessions as much as possible:

- Explore the physical space and the sensory space.

- Identify the local trees and plants.

- Observe which birds and animals share the space with you.

- Be aware of potential hazards, such as poisonous plants or fungi.

Find the natural resources which you can use in your sessions. Let the woods inspire you. As well as being useful in assessing what natural resources the site holds that you can make use of, this time exploring should help you to gain the sense of connection you are seeking to share with your learners.

Importance of time

As well as more physical space, Forest School's learner-led approach also provides more space in time. Much of the time a learner has the freedom to set the pace. The emphasis is on process rather than product. Fiona Hopkins, identifies 'enough time' as a key benefit of the Forest School pedagogy when she writes about inclusive practice[9] and Sara Knight states that:

> The importance of time in the learning process is often mentioned by teacher trainers but in the classrooms is usually ignored in favour of the importance of timetabled teaching… And yet, many of the case studies of Forest School activities cite time as the greatest gift the sessions bring… It would seem that in Forest School there is a pedagogy of time, a formal recognition of it's importance.[10]

Again, this approach can be naturally inclusive to autistic learners. We will discuss the importance of allowing processing time when communicating in the next chapter, but this awareness of having 'enough time' allows the learner this space to process when communicating. Learners have the time to attempt new experiences at their own pace, including the new experience of getting to know the practitioner. I have found that allowing the autistic people I have supported the time to get to know me at their own pace, avoiding unnecessary demands and pressures as far as possible, is a key component of building a trusting relationship. As well as having time to get to know the practitioner, the learner has the time to explore the physical space at their own pace, acclimatising themselves to the sensory and physical environment around them.

Some of my learners have initially sat and watched an activity for several sessions, interested but turning down offers to join in. As they have been able to see what is involved in their own time, without pressure to involve themselves until they have felt ready, they have been able to quietly build the confidence to take the first step of hands-on involvement. Getting to the point where they make that step has been a development target in itself and the first time that they chose to attempt the activity has been an achievement for the learner.

The three-way relationship between learner, practitioner and place does not need to be rushed. The most important initial target is the development of trust between all three partners in the relationship. This trust is the cornerstone of Forest School practice. Once you feel comfortable with each other, and with the place where sessions take place, then you can begin to grow and develop.

Learners

It is important to prepare your learners, and anyone who will accompany them, before they start to attend sessions. Do not lose sight of how difficult some people find it to begin a new activity. The better informed someone is, the more organised they will be. You are seeking to minimise stress caused by sudden surprises.

Think carefully about what someone needs to know beforehand and communicate this, as far as is possible, in a way that the autistic person will be able to understand. You should begin by finding out what they need to know by asking the person themselves and their support person.

- Would they like to be shown photographs of the site and staff? Or of the planned activities? Would they like to be told the planned structure of the session in advance and do they need photographs to support this?

- Do they require adjustments to be made to their structure in order to fit in with their own way of doing things?

- Agree on the format in which the information will be presented. Would the learner like a paper copy, a digital document or video? Would it be appropriate to present the information in an Easy Read format?

Try to ensure that the learner has had the chance to look over this information as much as possible beforehand, in their own time and with any necessary support. Be prepared to answer any questions and provide reassurance if they need it.

Things the learner will need to bring

Make sure that the learner, and whoever is accompanying them, knows what they will need to bring with them:

- Weather-appropriate clothing: layers, hats and boots in cold weather; light clothing in hot weather but long sleeves and trousers to discourage stings, scratches or insect bites, sun hats and suncream. You need to decide if you are going to provide waterproofs or if the learners should bring their own. It's useful to have some spare, just in case anyone does arrive without one. When I started providing Forest School I was shocked at how many of the support staff did not know how to dress to go outdoors! Be aware that some autistic people may have sensory issues that make it hard for them to wear some clothing – this will be discussed further in Chapter 8.

- The learner will need to make sure that any food and drink or medication they bring with them is stored in robust waterproof containers, which can be sealed to keep out bugs and rain.

Make sure that the learner, and anyone accompanying them, knows where you will meet, at what time and when the session will end. Make sure this information is clear and has been understood to avoid any last-minute panic or confusion which may get things off to a bad start.

Preparation moving forwards

Once the initial preparation is complete and sessions begin, the practitioner will start the process of making observations, building relationships and reflecting on how sessions are going.

For at least the first six sessions the practitioner's focus is usually on building the relationship between themselves, the learners and the woods. From the first session, boundaries are established, both the physical boundaries of the space which learners can safely explore, and acceptable boundaries of safe behaviour. Activities are planned which will encourage exploration and help the group to feel grounded in the place – sensory collecting activities, establishing a base camp. This period can go on for as long as the learners need it to. Allowing the time for this relationship to develop, for all parties to gain trust, is very important; Forest School seems to be more effective if it takes place over time, throughout the year.[11]

Development targets

The FSA Criteria for Good Practice state that: 'A Forest School programme has a structure which is based on the observations and collaborative work between learners and practitioners. This structure should clearly demonstrate progression of learning.' As the relationship between the learners, practitioners and place begins to grow, development targets can begin to be established.

The Forest School approach promotes holistic development and seeks to be relevant to the learner's home, work or school targets. In practice, this means planning sessions that tie in with curriculums, support plans or goals identified by the learner themselves. These targets may be specific to the learner, or apply to the whole group. If the practitioner is a member of the support or teaching staff, who provides Forest School as part of a wider job role, then they should already be aware of these targets. If the practitioner is not involved with the learners outside Forest School, they will need to liaise with any support staff, teachers or family in order to identify any targets for progression that they would like to be included in the Forest School programme.

Autistic learners may be involved with development programmes set up by other professionals, such as occupational therapists or speech and language therapists. The practitioner may need to liaise directly with these professionals, or via support staff, teachers or families, to learn how to incorporate these programmes in Forest School.

The most important voice in the process of establishing development targets is the learner themselves. With some autistic learners, the practitioner may find themselves receiving input from teachers, support staff, parents and other professionals. All of these people should be listened to, and viewed as partners in delivering positive outcomes for the learner, but it is vitally important that the practitioner does not ever lose sight of the need for practice to always be learner led.

The learner's choices should inform the direction their Forest School programme takes. In my opinion, an autistic person is never too young to begin to learn to self-advocate. Many of the barriers that autistic people face in their lives are caused by the assumptions of others, and an ability to assert your choices and needs is an invaluable skill. The greater the level of independence someone gains, the less support they will receive in explaining their needs to others. The ability to self-advocate can open opportunities in employment, education and social settings.

A trained practitioner will combine the feedback that the learner gives directly with observations of how they are interacting with the environment and group to identify development targets. By working in partnership with the learner, and place, the practitioner can individualise the programme to suit the needs of the learner. The practitioner will notice how the learner responds to the social, sensory and physical environment.

Often development targets become clear while observing sessions. A person might be drawn to working with fire. They may be fascinated by the combination of sensory stimuli (light, sound, heat, movement, smell) and the physical interaction (lighting, fuelling and then extinguishing the fire). The practitioner can use this focused interest to introduce lessons about social interaction and cooperating with others, such as taking turns to add more wood, working as a team to gather wood, communicating with others. Fine and gross motor skills, as well as exercise, can be encouraged by collecting wood and sawing or snapping kindling. Some learners will want to learn about the science that can explain fire, the process of wood dying and the changes that happen as it seasons which make it burn more easily. From this one simple activity there comes the potential to learn many different things, which can tie in with a development plan or curriculum, and the practitioner has been led here by the learner.

Autistic strengths

The Forest School approach seeks to use a learner-centred approach to identify and build a person's strengths. When working with autistic learners it is important to understand that many of their strengths exist because of their autism, not despite it. Being autism aware is not a case of ticking off a list of impairments. The practitioner should seek to learn how to identify and foster autism's strengths. Let's imagine we are foraging for food in the woods. We're looking for chicken-in-the-woods, a type of edible bracket fungus. Who do you want to help you? How about someone who naturally focuses on the details of what's around them, who notices patterns in the physical world? These are often autistic abilities and, in this context, they are definitely strengths.

Recognising autistic strengths is important. It's important for some autistic people, as they will be aware of their difference and will have a relationship with their autism. They are very conscious of their autism and how it affects their life. If someone can recognise that their autism, while bringing impairment and causing others to misunderstand them, also gives them strengths and abilities, then they can build a positive view of this aspect of themselves. The Forest School approach seeks to build resilience and self-esteem and gaining this self-acceptance is an important part of a person's development.

Some people may never conceptualise their autism in this way. It's just how their world is. It's still important for these people to have their strengths recognised. Inclusive practice seeks to value everyone taking part. Recognising people's ability is central to this. It's not only directly important for the person being valued, it is also important that they are valued by those around them. The individualised approach of Forest School, with its emphasis on recognising ability on the individual's terms and creating opportunities to achieve on those terms, gives learners the chance for their ability to be seen by peers, support staff and families.

Some autistic learners will rely on the support of others throughout their lives. It is vital that the people who provide this support respect and value the person receiving it. By creating opportunities for the person to show their strengths and abilities, by not focusing on impairment, the Forest School practitioner can help to reinforce the positive attitudes which the autistic person should expect from their support. For people who need to rely on support, the low expectations of others can disable them more than their autism. Forest School can play a part in challenging this, which can have a positive impact on the rest of the learner's life.

Making observations

Forest School practitioners are trained to make observations of their learners and how they interact with the world around them and with other people. These observations are used to develop individual programmes and to evidence growth and progression. When observing autistic learners, practitioners should pay attention to the same areas as they would with typical learners. Communication, confidence, fine and gross motor skills, independence, learning new skills – all of these areas of development can be observed. An autistic learner may show a difference in abilities in these areas but the Forest School approach recognises that all learners are different and will seek to develop the learner on an individual basis.

A key difference in the type of observation which may be made with autistic learners is the emphasis on sensory observation. Sensory issues will be discussed in more depth in Chapter 7. It is important that practitioners develop an awareness of how autistic people interact with their sensory environment as this can have a great impact on a person's well-being.

When making observations it's important not to begin from a point of assumption about the learner, whether that assumption is due to their autism or other factors. Work from what you are actually seeing. In *The Autistic Brain*, the well-known author Temple Grandin describes the 'bottom-up thinking' that autistic people display. This is the trait described as 'weak central coherence', that is: seeing the details rather than the bigger picture. Grandin discusses how this trait, often perceived as an impairment, can be a strength when analysing data. She suggests that neurotypical people will often decide on a hypothesis before looking for the data to support it, but autistic people will work with the data 'from the bottom up', that is, the data leads to the hypothesis.[12] This is definitely an example of an autistic approach that neurotypical practitioners should learn from. By concentrating on the detail of what you see, rather than working 'top down' from assumption, you will develop a better understanding of your learners.

Practitioners do not need to have a full understanding of everything they see their autistic learner do. Observations should be shared with the other people who are working in partnership to meet the learner's needs. The meaning of observations may not be apparent in the context of Forest School but may be very useful in the wider context of someone's support. People who have limited communication skills cannot always indicate exactly how they feel. Often issues with health or well-being only come to light from observations of a person made by different people over time. When other professionals, or family members, review the feedback which comes from Forest School it can help them to develop approaches or challenge assumptions.

Short-term targets

Development targets tend to be worked towards in the medium to long term. Sometimes the learner will arrive at a session with more immediate needs. The learner-led approach of Forest School allows the flexibility to accommodate this.

Again and again, the most valuable observations I make in my sessions happen when the learner is given the space to do their own thing. There is a structure there when learners need it and support is on hand to prompt and encourage, but when they seek activity on their own initiative, whether that is sensory, social or physical interactions, there is the potential for far greater insights than when someone is nagged to stay on a task that doesn't interest them.

Learners may have a strong need for sensory stimuli on a particular day. They are free to seek this and the chance to do so can help them to feel calm and to concentrate when they return to other settings after the session.

Learners may arrive feeling stressed due to things which have happened before Forest School. They may need the familiar structure of Forest School, or the time and space that Forest School can provide, to feel calm.

Some children may be in transition between homes or schools. At the times when these kind of life changes are happening, regular consistent activities, with predictable structures, are very important for helping someone adjust to the changes that are taking place in the rest of their lives.

Learners may just need to have fun. They may want to talk about their special interest or go through verbal routines or word play. They may want to return to a favourite activity which they have done before or just to sit and be still. The practitioner should not become inflexible when working towards targets. Never underestimate the positive benefits of having fun!

Staff development

Many autistic learners will attend Forest School with support. This may be a teaching assistant, support worker or family member. In my own practice, I involve the support staff in the session. I expect them to take part alongside the learner, rather than only stepping in at points when the learner needs support. Often support staff are outside their comfort zone and find that the learner is more able than they are in the situation. This experience can help to deepen their respect for the person they are supporting and make the learner's strengths more apparent than their impairments.

Forest School is a 'learning community where everybody has a stake in that learning – children, adult supporters and even landowners. Being learner centred therefore includes everyone...'[13]

The practitioner should be aware that any support staff or family members who attend along with the autistic learner can also benefit from the same learner-led approach. Building the confidence and self-esteem of supporters and encouraging good practice should always be part of the development targets for the group.

Reflection

The Forest School approach encourages reflection as part of the learning process. Sessions often have a structured time to reflect and share ideas with the group. This often happens at the end of a session when the group comes together to sit and share food and a drink. This time encourages the group to take ownership of the Forest School experience and their own development.

Autistic learners may require accommodations to be made to help them to take part in this time. Consider how to best facilitate communication on the learner's own terms. Consider if the learner wants to communicate at this time. Some learners may find it easier to complete a brief questionnaire after each session, for some it may be better to give the chance to give feedback on a one-to-one basis during the session or afterwards, for some contributing their feedback to the rest of the group could be an appropriate development target. The practitioner needs to be sensitive to the balance between giving the learner the chance to take ownership of their experience in this way and the social anxiety which it can cause, and adjust approaches as required.

Support staff are also encouraged to reflect on their role within the group and practice and this benefits both the person whom they are supporting and their own professional development.

Practitioners who come from a background in social care or education will already be aware of the importance of developing reflective practice. The ongoing awareness and analysis of one's own practice is an important factor in improving the quality of service and closing the gap between theory and practice. This emphasis on ongoing learning and improvement is another case of the Forest School approach running in parallel with existing best practice for providing support for autistic people. Practitioners reflect on the development of individual learners, group dynamics, development targets and their own effectiveness and these insights help to facilitate the direction and development of the sessions.

KEY POINTS

▶ Inclusion is the practice of making sure that everyone, regardless of any perceived differences, is valued and can take part in society.

▶ Inclusive practice makes accommodations for an individual's needs but recognises that sometimes a person may not be able to take part in every activity. In this case, a choice of activities, *of equal appeal and value to the whole group,* should be offered.

▶ A person with a perceived disability experiences the same benefits overcoming achievable challenges as any other person.

▶ Autistic people like to have a clear and consistent structure and this should always be planned into sessions. However, a practitioner should remember to be led by the learner and sensitive to how much an individual is actually using the structure. If they are being consistently flexible, then you can be.

▶ Autistic people may show strength in systemising. The practitioner should be aware of what this is and try to think in terms of systems when planning sessions and building their relationship with an autistic learner.

▶ Before starting a course of sessions, the practitioner should find out about the learner's individual needs:

• health issues

- dietary requirements

- mobility/physical requirements

- communication

- sensory profile

- behavioural support

- likes and dislikes.

▶ Initial development targets concentrate on building a relationship between learners, practitioners and place.

▶ Autistic people are often more engaged in the physical than social world and may have heightened sensory sensitivity. The importance placed on the physical environment in the Forest School approach can encourage an autism-inclusive approach.

▶ The Forest School approach allows learners more time than many other settings, which can be beneficial to autistic learners.

▶ The practitioner must make sure that the learner, or their support staff, is thoroughly aware of what to bring with them to Forest School. Expectations need to be clear from the outset and the practitioner should be prepared to give information and offer reassurance.

▶ Forest School strives to be a holistic part of someone's overall growth and development. Practitioners may develop targets for the learner with input from teachers, families, support staff or other professionals but it is important that the key stakeholder in developing targets is the learner themselves.

▶ The practitioner should always be aware of the learner's strengths and understand that some of these strengths arise because of the learner's autism, not despite it. It is important that the practitioner develops a positive attitude towards autism rather than only being aware of the impairments it may cause.

▶ Observations are made to build up understanding of learners and develop individualised learning programmes. Observations made at Forest School should not be based on 'top-down' assumptions. Observations should be shared, when appropriate, with other stakeholders and can be important in informing the 'bigger picture' of a person's needs.

▶ The learner-led approach gives people the chance to take what they need from a session. Sometimes a learner may need to satisfy sensory needs, socialise or have quiet space. Session plans are flexible and can accommodate this. The observations made when learners act on their own initiative often contain the most important insights.

▶ The Forest School approach recognises that everyone, including practitioners, is a learner and encourages reflection and learning for all attending.

CHAPTER 5

Communication

All autistic people experience some level of difficulty with communication and social interaction. Communication refers to the message that a person receives or sends to others, and social interaction is the reciprocal responses to these messages.

Differences in self-expression and understanding others present a significant challenge to autistic people, and the autism-aware practitioner must learn how to communicate and interact with the learner. Keep in mind that the practitioner will need to learn to communicate on the learner's terms. If the autistic person could easily communicate on neurotypical terms they probably wouldn't have been diagnosed with an ASD.

The preferred communication styles of autistic people can be very individualised. In my sessions with more significantly impaired learners it is usual for each to have quite distinct, and different, styles of communication. Forest School's learner-led ethos, with its emphasis on establishing trust, observing an individual's learning style and the practitioner being open to learning themselves, is well suited to accommodating the person-centred approach required to interact with autistic people. In order to achieve this, the practitioner needs to develop an awareness of how the autistic person communicates, and to reflect on how they communicate themselves. The advice in this chapter can only give a generalised overview and further reading and direct observation are essential. For people unused to communicating in different ways, trying to interact with an autistic person can be quite a daunting prospect but

I can honestly say that many of the most enlightening and fun social interactions I've had have been with autistic people.

Barriers to communication

On a practical level, the practitioner must consider what the barriers to communication are in their interaction with an autistic learner. Awareness of what the barriers are to begin with will help to focus the practitioner on what needs to be done to overcome them. It's important to reflect on the extent that these barriers are being created by the practitioner themselves in their usual communication style and their assumptions about how this style is being understood by others.

Attention and focus

This is a good point to begin because if you don't have the attention of the autistic person in the first place, communication is likely to fail. Difficulty in maintaining joint attention is one of the earliest indicators of autism. An autism-aware practitioner needs to be sensitive to the differences in executive function which can make it hard for the autistic person to shift attention as quickly as a neurotypical person may. The practitioner also needs to consider that in a neurotypical interaction people are hardwired to respond more to the human face and voice than the objects around them but that this is not always the case for autistic people.[1] This means you may not actually be of more natural interest to the person with whom you are trying to communicate than the bark on the tree they are looking at. Don't try to convey the important part of your message to the person until you have gained their attention. Be patient if this doesn't happen as quickly as you'd normally expect.

Reflect on your own communication and always question if you are presenting the information to the autistic person in a way in which they are most likely to be able to take it in. Always be prepared to learn how to change the way information is presented if necessary.

Processing time

The autistic brain processes things in a different way to the typical brain. For some things, such as pattern recognition or attention to detail, the autistic brain may be more naturally efficient than a typical brain, but for some other things, such as processing social input from others, the autistic brain may need a little more time to respond.

Neurotypical people naturally edit the input which their brain is receiving from the world around them. The senses feed in the data and the brain quickly sorts through it all, prioritising to establish a bigger picture. Autistic people describe this process as often taking conscious effort. The information is flooding in but they need longer to prioritise which data to focus on and don't automatically edit to receive the bigger picture.[2]

The practitioner will need to be aware that the person they are communicating with is processing things differently and adjust their own pace and style of interaction to accommodate this. They need to allow time for a person to respond. This can feel strange at first as the practitioner may be conditioned to operate at a neurotypical pace in interactions. Autistic people sometimes describe communicating with neurotypicals as an intellectual process. Responses that just flow straight along for neurotypical people require active consideration. It is like trying to understand someone speaking in a foreign language. This responsibility should not fall entirely on the autistic person. The practitioner should be trying to adjust their pace and style of communication to make it easier to understand and to leave enough space for the response to be properly considered. At the beginning of my career, I had to consciously learn to stop myself from rephrasing whatever I had said when a response had not come as quickly as I expected. Although this helped me when communicating with other neurotypicals, it was a terrible way to communicate with autistic people who had probably only just come to the end of processing my first statement and thinking how to respond before I threw another one at them and took them back to square one!

Sensory barriers

The practitioner needs to be aware that the sensory input being experienced may be being processed very differently by the autistic learner. This may be occurring over more than one sensory domain.

Differences in auditory processing can have a significant impact on verbal interaction. Autistic people can find it difficult to process verbal communication because they are finding it hard to focus on the communication more than the background noise. Temple Grandin describes having difficulty in hearing hard consonants as a child.[3] This sensitivity may fluctuate and can lead to concerns that the person may be deaf.[4]

Heightened sensory input can become very distracting, either through causing discomfort or fascination, and, once distracted, autistic people can find it very difficult to shift their attention back to the social interaction on which they are being expected to focus.

Some autistic people describe using only one modality at a time to process sensory input. This is called monoprocessing, or monotropism, and means that someone is only consciously taking in the input from one of their senses at a time – for example, if they are thinking about what they can see, they cannot simultaneously think about what they can hear. This can apply across all the senses. If someone is engrossed in exploring an object through touch they may not be ignoring your verbal communication but rather it is in a queue to be processed and has not entered into their conscious consideration yet.[5]

The practitioner needs to consider whether they are creating the sensory barrier themselves. Speaking loudly or with a high pitch, the smell of deodorant or woodsmoke, patterned clothing – these types of sensory input, which you may be unwittingly causing, can impact significantly on the learner's ability to focus on communication.

An autism-aware practitioner needs to consider how the environment is affecting the efficacy of their communication. This will tie in with attention and processing. Keep in mind the phrase 'too much information'. This is what we want to avoid! The practitioner needs to try to develop sensitivity to how much is going on in the autistic person's head. If the autistic person's responses are slowing or they look distracted, then attempts at communication are adding more input into a situation that is becoming overloaded. If communication is necessary at this point, it should be simplified as much as possible. The best way to do this depends on the individual learner but the most common approach is to use visual forms of communication.

Stress levels

Stress has a significant impact on the lives of many autistic people. The practitioner must be aware that the underlying baseline level of stress is often significantly higher for an autistic person than for a neurotypical person. Helping to manage stress is a key part of supporting autistic people.

If a person's stress level is rising this can significantly affect their ability to communicate. At some point in our lives we all experience heightened stress levels. It is worth reflecting on how this affects your own communication. Do you become more reasonable? Better at listening to others? More considered in your responses? I would hazard a guess that the answer to those questions is in the negative.

If an autistic person is experiencing a rising level of stress, their thinking is likely to become more rigid and inflexible and they will find it harder to process your communication and respond appropriately. The practitioner must learn to be sensitive to the autistic person's level of stress and be aware that a person will communicate better when they feel calmer in themselves. Unless whatever you are trying to communicate absolutely has to be said that second, the priority should be giving the autistic person the time and space to feel calm before continuing to communicate.

Methods of communication

Throughout this book I emphasise how broad a diagnosis autism is. I dislike the terms 'high' or 'low' functioning because I feel that they come laden with assumptions about the capability of the person they are describing.

Over the course of my career I have met people with a diagnosis of ASD and moderate learning disability who have excellent life skills when it comes to caring for themselves and their apartment and carrying out a job for others. I have also met people with a diagnosis of Asperger syndrome who have struggled to maintain the most basic levels of personal hygiene, whose lack of housekeeping skills made their home environment quite dangerous and whose high levels of stress made employment impossible (I should add that I have also met plenty of neurotypical people who would also fit this description!). The latter would be described as higher functioning according to this terminology but the former are probably more functional in practical terms and may present as having a greater level of well-being.

Possibly one of the strongest assumptions made about autistic people stems from the level to which that person uses language to communicate. That is, that the use of language in verbal or written communication is the most reliable indicator of the person's ability to understand social interactions. This assumption can be very misleading in a way that misjudges both autistic people who use verbal language as their main method of communication and those who do not.

There are two distinct and interconnected parts to language skills – *expressive* and *receptive*. Receptive language skills are the ability to *understand* language, while expressive skills are the ability to *use* language to communicate.

People with a diagnosis of Asperger syndrome are often very articulate when expressing themselves and this leads to an assumption that their ability to process receptive language is not impaired. However, it is often the ability to process incoming communication which is most difficult for these people, and the person communicating with them needs to be more aware of how to make accommodations in their own communication style to help to overcome this.

Conversely, people who are limited in their use of expressive language often have stronger skills in receptive language than people communicating with them assume. Sadly, it is not uncommon for people to discuss an autistic person, who doesn't use verbal language to communicate as if they were not there, when those who know them will be aware that they understand most of what is said around them.

Verbal communication

The extent to which verbal communication is used by autistic people varies a great deal. Generally, neurotypical people rely on verbal communication to express needs, ideas and feelings to one another. Face-to-face verbal communication is emphasised by the use of body language and tone of voice. Facial expression and tone of voice can completely change the meaning of words spoken. The same phrase can be changed from high praise to mocking sarcasm with the raising of an eyebrow and a slight change in pitch. Neurotypical people often like to use idioms and turns of phrase.

Autistic people often miss the subtler meanings carried by body language and tone of voice and so prefer language to be used literally. Idioms are confusing if you try to understand them literally. Try the phrase 'raining cats and dogs'. It sounds quite charming to neurotypical ears, perhaps like a description of a rain shower from a nursery rhyme. Try interpreting it literally and the idea of pets falling from the skies sounds as if it comes straight from one of the scarier passages in the Book of Revelation.

Tony Attwood describes the conversational style he has developed over many years of interacting with people with Asperger syndrome as 'Aspergerese'.[6] This is a good way for the practitioner to think about their interactions with an autistic learner as it focuses on the need for communication to be considered, as you would do if speaking in another language.

Tips for verbal communication

- *Use literal language* – The practitioner should use direct, literal language and avoid phrases and idioms that may cause confusion. If giving instruction, use as few words as possible and reinforce them with body language, such as pointing at what you are talking about or passing a tool to the person, if appropriate. If the learner is accompanied to the sessions by someone who already knows them, observe their interaction and learn how the person prefers to communicate.

- *Be honest and straightforward* – The practitioner should ensure that they are honest and straightforward when communicating. Neurotypical communication sometimes relies on saying one thing with words but communicating the opposite with tone of voice and subtle body language. Often this is done out of a sense of politeness in an attempt to 'let someone down gently' – for instance, saying, 'We'll do that later, maybe' while actually meaning, 'I have no intention whatsoever of doing that today but don't want to make you feel rejected.' Autistic people will often say exactly what they mean without sugarcoating it. This level of honesty can seem abrupt and rude but remember that this is seldom the intention. Say what you mean in an unequivocal way and do not make promises you don't intend to keep.

- *Be explicit* – Don't assume that the person you are speaking to will pick up subtle implicit signals during the interaction. State things in a clear and explicit way. For instance, if someone is continuing to speak to you when you need to direct your attention elsewhere then you will need to say explicitly, 'I have to stop our conversation now because I have to help John light the fire. I can speak about this with you again when we stop for a drink at two o'clock.' It can help to be clear about when the conversation or activity can happen again. Some people can think that the end of an activity or conversation means that it won't ever happen again and this may cause stress. Stating clearly (and honestly!) when it can happen again can be reassuring. This is particularly the case if someone is talking about a special interest. Some people will need to go back to the beginning of whatever they were telling you if they are stopped mid-flow and, in some cases, they may find it very difficult to move on if a verbal exchange hasn't been completed in the way they were expecting it to. Knowledge of the individual needs to guide you as to the appropriate strategy to move on the conversation.

- *Listen* – This ought to go without saying. Unfortunately, I have witnessed neurotypical people ignoring clear communication from an autistic person more times than I can count. Inevitably this leads to frustration on the part of the autistic person and sometimes this is expressed in challenging behaviour. If someone tells you that they need help or don't like something then listen to them and help them to resolve the situation. Make sure that the learner has the opportunity to express themselves on their own terms.

- *Be sensitive to how the learner is feeling* – Are they particularly enjoying what they're doing? Can they express what it is that they find enjoyable in the activity? The emphasis on observation of individual learners, which is inherent in the Forest School approach, lends itself again to the need for awareness of the individual, which lies at the heart of meeting the needs of an autistic learner.

Echolalia

Some autistic people repeat words or phrases they have heard. Sometimes words are repeated immediately after they are heard and sometimes there is a delay and they are repeated some time after being heard. This is called echolalia.

Sometimes echolalia has a communicative function but sometimes the function is non-communicative.

Communicative immediate echolalia may be used to help process what has been said and create more time for a response to be decided on. Some people may use an echolalic response as a request or as an answer to a request, for instance a learner saying, 'Do you want a hot chocolate?' may mean, 'I would like a hot chocolate.'

Learners with delayed communicative echolalia may use words or phrases heard in the past to communicate in the present. Sometimes the phrase used may not seem to be relevant to the current situation. For instance, one of the men who attends my sessions will say, '– is not going on a boat'. There is no possibility of ever going on a boat during his session, but this phrase is used to indicate that he is worried, and needs reassurance about what is happening now and next. Although you need to ensure that you use literal language when you communicate with an autistic learner, some learners may be using these type of non-literal phrases to communicate with you. This type of communication will be individual and you will need to learn what the different phrases mean and what responses are expected.

Sometimes echolalia is not intended as communication and is used playfully, with pleasure being taken in the feel and sound of the words and phrases or playing back social interactions or TV shows which the person has enjoyed in the past. Sometimes the person may be playing back previous experiences which were stressful and speaking out loud as they process them. Sometimes the person may be repeating phrases or words that hold associations for them relating to their current situation. For instance, a woman who attends my sessions says, 'What does the goat do?' when she walks past an area where she used to come to feed a (long since disappeared!) goat.

Repetitive phrases: systems and games

This use of repetitive phrases to communicate is often an invitation for interaction, with the person expecting a set response to different phrases. In my practice, I interpret this as a system that has been developed by the autistic person themselves to facilitate communication with others. Different phrases have different meanings and functions. Sometimes the person may just want to interact with you and make small talk. Sometimes a set phrase may have another meaning, such as the example of 'the boat' which I mentioned above. By giving the correct responses that the person expects to hear, you create a predictable system of communication that reassures the person and gives them responses that are easier to process. It is important to learn these systems, as giving the wrong response can cause stress. This also relates to trigger words, which can cause a person immediate stress if heard. To return to the example I used earlier, the word 'boat' would trigger stress in the man concerned. It is important to remember that it may be the actual word, and not its meaning, that would trigger this response in many cases. Different words with the same meaning (such as ship, canoe, raft) would not elicit the same response.

Some autistic people love word games, enjoying the sound and feel of different words or the repetition of familiar sequences of phrases. Some neurotypical people can find these repetitive exchanges quite wearing but I have to confess that I thoroughly enjoy them, and see them as a good way to bond with the people who use them at my sessions.

I have met very articulate people with Asperger syndrome who have created their own, complex, repetitive communication systems. A good example of this was a young man who would engage each new person whom he met in a debate about an ethical belief which was important to him. His argument was carefully scripted and he would ask the same questions and state the same points, in the same order, each time. The different responses of the people he ran through this system would help him to get a measure of who they were and how he felt about them. The new person often wasn't aware of the repetitive nature of the exchange until they saw him run the next new person through his system.

Written communication

Written communication, whether freehand or typed, is used by many autistic people to communicate. Written language is shared with the general population and is easily understood by most neurotypical people. There are many accomplished autistic writers whose work is available both in print and online, and many autistic people make use of online forums to communicate with others using the written word. Arguably, the use of written communication is increasing in the general population as technology encourages communication on social media and via text messaging.

Written language is a medium that can suit autistic people very well as it can be processed at their own pace and is divorced from the need to simultaneously try to pick up signals from body language and tone of voice. To avoid confusion, it is still important to ensure that any communication you make in written language is clear, unambiguous and literal.

Written language can be presented together with pictures or 'widgets' to make it easier to understand. Widgets are symbols that have been developed to support the written word. Words and phrases will have a widget symbol to represent them, together with the written word. Widgets are used to produce Easy Read documents, which are often used to present information to people who benefit from this approach. Widgets frequently appear in visual timetables to support a person in sequencing their day and making choices. The practitioner should ask if this way of presenting information is used by the learner and consider how to utilise it if it is. Schools and services that use widgets should be able to help the practitioner to produce Easy Read documents if they are required, or to supply widgets that are relevant to Forest School to include on visual schedules or choice boards.

Social Stories™

Social Stories™ were developed by Carol Gray in 1991. Social Stories™ are simple sequenced stories that relate to a particular situation or event and contain advice on how to respond appropriately. They can be used to teach skills such as self-care, to reinforce social skills, provide positive feedback, cope with stressful events and so on. They are written in a format that will best suit the person they are created for. Existing Social Stories™ may be used at Forest School if they are relevant in that setting, or Social Stories™ may be produced especially for Forest School sessions. An example of this would be a Social Story™ to reinforce safety when having a campfire if there had been concerns about a learner's behaviour around the fire. The Social Story™ should be written by someone who understands the person, their autism and how to write this kind of story.[7]

Communication systems

Some autistic people make use of communication systems that have been developed to be used by people who have disabilities which impair their ability to use the more commonly used methods of communication.

These methods of communication are sometimes more meaningful for the autistic person. Olga Bogdashina writes about the way that autistic people may develop their own inner language based on sensory experience. These inner languages are perceptually based, rather than meaning based as verbal language is. Bogdashina describes these as visual, auditory, tactile, kinaesthetic, olfactory and gustatory languages.[8] By using communication systems that relate better to these perceptual inner languages we can present communication in a way that is more naturally processed by the autistic person.

These communication systems are learned by the autistic person, usually in tandem with attempting to learn the commonly used methods of communication (verbal and written), if they have shown a significant delay in developing typical communication. For some autistic people, these systems are an important method of communication and when this is the case, it is important that the practitioner makes the effort to learn them.

Commonly used systems include:

- *MAKATON* – This involves 'signing' in a similar way to sign languages used by the deaf (many MAKATON signs are taken from deaf sign languages such as British Sign Language). MAKATON was developed for use by people with learning disabilities but is also used widely in early years settings. MAKATON communication is received visually and expressed kinaesthetically.

- *PECS (Picture Exchange Communication System)* – This is a communication system in which pictures of objects are used to express a person's choices or needs. The pictures are often kept in a file and are small and laminated; they are taken out by the person and shown (often by being put on a velcro strip on plastic backing) to whoever they are trying to communicate with. If a learner uses PECS to communicate, the practitioner should make sure that they have the PECS symbols which they will need to make choices during Forest School (this may involve introducing new symbols).

- *Apps* – At this point I am prepared for some Forest School practitioners to throw their hands up in horror at my heresy! For many people, Forest School is about getting learners away from technology, particularly if that technology has a screen! However, it is important to acknowledge how useful technology can be in providing ways for people to communicate who would otherwise struggle. There are many different apps available to help autistic people communicate, some are digital versions of some of the systems we have already discussed and others use different systems. In this case, the presence of a tablet in the woods should be viewed in the same way as you would view a hearing aid or pair of spectacles. Some learners may benefit from having a digital introduction to Forest School, perhaps a digital video introducing them to the site and the practitioner.

Other methods of communication

Some autistic people are very limited in their use of learned methods of communication to express themselves. They rely instead on body language, verbal noises, pointing or leading people to things they require, making associations with objects, sensory interactions (such as squeezing arms) and, if very stressed, presenting challenging behaviour.

Some of these communications are easy to understand, such as smiling when happy, or grimacing and biting their own hand when frustrated. Others can be very subtle, such as looking briefly at something that they would like you to pass to them. The practitioner must take care to learn these individualised languages, from the learner themselves and from those who already know them. The learner-led approach of Forest School, with its emphasis on individualised observation and reflection, lends itself well to the approaches required when getting to know people who use these idiosyncratic communication methods. It is important to reiterate the earlier point that use of expressive verbal language does not necessarily correlate with understanding of receptive verbal language.

When considering the different ways that autistic people communicate you should also reflect on the ways in which you communicate yourself. It's likely that you use different methods to communicate over the course of a typical day, depending on the situation. Over one day, I use verbal language, body language, written communication, emails, my phone, and touch, when I cuddle up to my family. It is the same for autistic people and you need to consider which of the methods of communication they use best suits the current interaction. This can particularly apply if you are trying to communicate with someone who is becoming stressed.

Finally, I would advise practitioners who are just beginning to work with autistic people to not be too hard on themselves when they make mistakes. The Forest School pedagogy recognises that the practitioner is a learner too and this is very much the case when communicating with autistic people. You are learning a new way to interact with others and each autistic person you meet may have quite different things to teach you. It's not easy and you will make mistakes. Please remember the old saying, 'If you don't make mistakes, you don't make anything.' Mistakes are lessons. Reflect on them, learn from them and come back ready to do it better. One of the great pleasures of working with autistic people is the satisfaction which comes from learning to communicate with each other.

KEY POINTS

▶ All autistic people present a level of impairment in communication and social interaction. Communication refers to the message that a person receives or sends to others. Social interaction is the reciprocal responses to these messages.

▶ The practitioner will need to learn to communicate on the learner's terms and these can be very different from one autistic person and another.

▶ Before attempting to communicate, the practitioner should consider if there are any barriers to communication present. These may include: having the person's attention, differences in processing times, differences in sensory processing and if the autistic person is feeling stressed.

▶ We all use different methods of communication at different times. When communicating with autistic people we need to discover which methods suit them best at different times and use these. This may involve modifying how we communicate or learning entirely new ways to communicate.

▶ Autistic people may use verbal language to communicate but are likely to have differences in how they understand others and express themselves. Use straightforward and literal language, allow processing time, avoid idioms and do not make assumptions about understanding based on the way that the autistic person expresses themselves verbally. Most importantly: *listen!*

▶ Some autistic people use set phrases and verbal routines to communicate. These can seem odd and it may not be immediately apparent what they mean but they have a function. It's important to learn what different phrases mean and what responses (if any) are expected.

▶ Autistic people may prefer to use different methods of communication which are easier for them to understand. Some, such as written communication, are shared with most neurotypical people while others, such as sign language or written widget symbols, need to be learned by the practitioner.

▶ Some autistic people may not express themselves with languages or systems that are used widely by others. However, they will still communicate through body language and actions and it is important that the practitioner recognises this. It is also very important that the practitioner realises that a person's use of expressive communication does not necessarily correlate with their understanding of received communication.

CHAPTER 6

Social Interaction

Forest School contains a strong social dimension. Sessions tend to be attended by groups and social interaction is an important part of the process. Most autistic people find unstructured social interaction challenging to some extent, and it's common for autistic children to find the social free for all of school break the most stressful part of the day.

In the previous chapter, we considered the different ways that autistic people communicate and the need for a conscious effort to be made when neurotypical people interact with autistic people. It's important to reflect on how much more difficult this is when the autistic person has to interact within a group, with more people talking, more people using body language and tone of voice, the pace of interaction and social cues increasing. For someone who may need to make a conscious effort to process all of these things, interacting within groups can be a daunting prospect.

The learner-led approach recognises that different participants will benefit from different aspects of Forest School and is flexible in meeting their needs. A learner-led approach allows the people who come to Forest School to take ownership of the experience and to show the practitioner what they need to take from their sessions. The sensitive practitioner should learn what the learner's needs are and how best to support them.

For some autistic learners, developing social skills and strategies may be one of the development targets to work towards, for others Forest School may give the learner the opportunity to reduce social demands while gaining other benefits, such as learning new practical skills or taking the opportunity to regulate sensory processing. Many learners may seek all of these things over the course of a single session, at their own pace and as they need to.

For a practical example of a Forest School session, consider Jon Cree's account of the session which he describes here:

> A visiting practitioner to a teenage Forest School group was the catalyst for a memorable example of this for me. The group wanted to play catch the flag, again!, and began a pregame negotiation that ended up lasting some forty-five minutes. During this time, the visitor interjected a number of times, saying, 'no, this is the way to play this game', 'lets get playing', and 'when will you guys start playing?!' I was sorely tempted to say 'we're already playing', but bit my lip as I didn't want to humiliate. One of the boys turned and explained, 'once we have all decided how we are going to play this it will make it so much more fun and all of us who want to will join in properly.'
>
> Yet more proof, for me, that as practitioners we need to question our own urges, sit back, and make space for and be attentive to the declarations, questions and gifts each learner brings forward. In terms of learner-centred processes, the key phrases in this group member's response were 'once we have all' and 'all of us who want to'. The playing was in the negotiation as well as the game, and the learning was all the deeper for it; the depth and creativity was in the divergent thinking and chat in the negotiation as well as in the physical act of the game, its tactics and problem solving.
>
> An atmosphere of 'we are all in this together' was prevalent, and for those that didn't want to engage in catch the flag, that was fine, they were still 'in this together'. They could pursue their own interests, indeed a couple of boys were keen during this session to continue making their own chairs and one girl carried on constructing hammock. By 'in this together' I meant we all agreed we could learn and pursue our own agendas providing it didn't disrupt others' learning processes.[1]

This account perfectly illustrates the learner-led approach in practice. We can see how easily this approach accommodates the needs of different learners in the session. Consider the choices that different learners are making. There is a choice between taking part in the social interaction of the group negotiation, with the potential lessons of listening to different points of view, patience, turn taking and compromising to reach a shared goal. However, it's recognised as equally valid to choose to work in a pair constructing chairs or to choose to pursue an activity alone and carry on working on a hammock. We can see the potential for autistic learners to choose whichever activity best suits them at the time or to seek a different activity altogether.

Once again, we can see how the Forest School approach, if guided by an autism-aware practitioner, has the potential to provide inclusive opportunities. Any interventions to support social interaction which are in place in other settings can be carried into Forest School and incorporated into Forest School development targets.

In Chapter 4, we discussed how one of the strengths of the Forest School approach is the space in time which it affords. Learners can engage at their own pace and practitioners can show flexibility in the level of demand placed on an individual learner. This approach understands and respects difference and can give the autistic learner the chance to interact on their own terms and at their own pace – it's okay to sit and watch or to seek solitary activities.

Principle 5 of the FSA Criteria for Good Practice states that there should be a high ratio of practitioners/adults to learners. This can benefit those learners who prefer one-to-one social interaction as there should be practitioners or support staff present who have the time to give these learners the attention they require to get the most from their sessions.

Forest School provides great opportunities to share positive experiences with others. Experiences such as taking turns on rope swings, working as a team to build something or to cook a meal, sharing shelter during a rain shower or sitting around a fire on a frosty morning drinking hot chocolate are natural social experiences. Shared experiences give us a connection to others that does not have to involve direct communication. Sometimes differences in sensory processing, or difficulty in maintaining joint attention, may mean that an autistic learner is not experiencing something in the same way as the other people with them, but this will not always be the case. Creating the opportunity for someone to share these experiences, in their own way and in a nurturing environment, can have a positive impact not only for the autistic learner but also for all members of the group, including practitioners and supporters. Creating a nurturing social environment where people can feel relaxed, free from judgement of any differences and are able to be themselves should be a priority when reflecting on how to create an autism-inclusive session.

Roles and rules

All social groups assign roles to the individuals in the group and rules for their behaviour to some extent. Autistic people sometimes learn to navigate social situations by learning these rules and roles, but tend to be rigid and inflexible in their understanding of them. The practitioner needs to be aware that rules and roles can be a great way to build the confidence of autistic learners when interacting with the group but that once they are accepted, changes or inconsistency can cause stress.

Some roles may take place every session, such as being the person who carries the kelly kettles to site, while others may be specific to the activity taking place, like being the person who chops the onions in a particular cooking session.

If the roles are repeated over sessions this can be a good way for the learner to take ownership of their session, build trust and take the opportunity to show responsibility and capability. Feeling that your role is valued and being thanked and praised for your contribution boosts self-esteem. Consider before assigning regular roles if they are going to be shared. If they are, then be clear from the outset that turns are taken and explain when the learner can expect to take their next turn. Don't suddenly decide that someone else is going to take over the role which the autistic learner has been carrying out as this could be confusing and interpreted as a negative judgement.

Forest School sessions involve activities that can carry a level of risk, and safety boundaries are put in place from the outset. It is very important when setting these boundaries that the practitioner is consistent in how they are interpreted from then on. Telling the group that they are not to eat anything from the woods one week, and several weeks later foraging for blackberries, is only going to cause confusion. Some autistic people are vociferous in demanding that rules are followed precisely by other people (while often not being so strict when following the rules themselves). This can lead to conflict with others who may feel that the law should be interpreted in spirit rather than to the letter. It's important to consider this from the perspective of the autistic person – they are not being pedantic to dominate others, even if it may seem this way. If you find it hard to predict and interpret the behaviour of people around you then you may wish that other people follow a concrete system of rules that introduce some boundaries and predictability to their behaviour. As the practitioner, if you consider it from this angle perhaps you'll also be more forgiving if you sometimes observe a little hypocrisy in the learner in regard to how rules are applied to others and how they apply them to themselves!

Autism and play

Although Forest School is suitable for all ages, the majority of UK sessions are predominantly provided for children. The Forest School approach encourages learning through play, and research suggests that play in a natural environment stimulates physical fitness,[2] improved balance and motor skills[3] and improved outcomes in social interaction.[4]

When considering how to provide Forest School to autistic children the practitioner needs to be aware of the differences in play between these children and their neurotypical peers.

Children learn about the world through play and typically progress from early functional play, learning how objects function, through to creative and imaginative play when objects are used in symbolic ways (e.g. using a branch to symbolise a horse which a child is riding). Typical children engage with other people through play and act out social situations, often adopting pretend roles.

As we have discussed in earlier chapters, autistic people perceive the world in a different way from their typically developing peers and this is reflected in how they engage in play activities. Children with ASD may play with objects in a non-functional way, for example running the wheel of a toy car repetitively along their arm, or they may not want to engage in playing with toys with other people.[5] They have difficulty with the symbolic aspects of play and when they do pretend play it is often in ways that typical peers find hard to understand. They may be quite rigid and controlling when acting out scenes involving favourite fictional characters[6] and, in some cases, may role play by pretending to be favourite objects.[7]

Some research suggests that learning to play on neurotypical terms may contribute to better outcomes in later developmental abilities of cognition and language.[8] Interventions such as JASPER (Joint Attention, Symbolic Play and Regulation) are used to encourage reciprocal play and symbolic play. In the context of Forest School, the practitioner should be working in partnership with the learner's supporters to include any such interventions in sessions.

A very interesting intervention from the point of view of running inclusive Forest School sessions is Integrated Play Group (IPG).[9] This approach encourages child-led play in groups that include both autistic and neurotypical children. Crucially, IPG seeks to teach the neurotypical children how better to understand their autistic playmates as well as vice versa. IPG is aimed at children between 3 and 11 years old, but a programme for teens and adults (ITSG) is also being used. Research[10] shows that this approach leads to improvements in play and social skills. The ethos of IPG, which involves teaching neurotypical peers how to play better with autistic children, is worth incorporating into Forest School sessions whether the intervention is being followed or not. This approach is the foundation of establishing inclusivity.

As well as considering how autistic people can learn to play on neurotypical terms, it's important to learn how to recognise when autistic people are playing on their own terms. As we have mentioned, play is a pleasurable way in which children learn about the world. In previous chapters, we have discussed some of the ways in which autistic perceptions of the world differ from the neurotypical experience. Learning about the social world is a big motivator in neurotypical play but it's not the only way that typical children play. My own children like to seek sensory experiences such as swinging and spinning or sliding in the playpark. Children like playing alone building LEGO® structures, or taking things apart to see how they work. Go to your local toy store and see how many things there are designed for play that isn't necessarily social or symbolic. My daughter often comes home from school and sings songs to herself that she has learned in class. She seems to take pleasure in the sounds and has rote learned the lyrics. This is all play, and it is play that autistic people will initiate to varying extents.

In Chapter 4 we mentioned how some autistic people may live more in the physical world than the social world. The physical world and the world of sensory perception are arguably more real than the social world, which tends to preoccupy many neurotypical people. Many autistic people not only derive pleasure from exploring the physical and sensory world but learn valuable skills. Allow your learners the space to play in their own ways and to build their strengths as well as being aware of their impairments.

Remember too, Temple Grandin's phrase 'An anthropologist on Mars'. Sometimes autistic people learn through setting themselves apart a little and studying others. Try to recognise when this is happening. One man who attended my sessions sat and watched for several months. He always chose to come along with his group but politely declined all offers to join in with the activities. Then one day he suddenly decided that he had watched enough and began to volunteer himself for different tasks and take part with the others. I have no idea of what process was taking place over the months of watching, but by not overly pressuring this learner, we gave him the space to allow whatever had to happen to happen.

Initiating action: prompts and transitions

Some autistic learners may find it hard to judge when to begin or end an activity and this can lead to stress when transitioning between activities. Different strategies are used to help a person with these transitions. Sometimes these may be part of an intervention programme such as TEACHH[11] or SCERTS,[12] sometimes they may be completely individualised. It's important that the practitioner is aware of what strategies are used. If strategies are in place that require visual representations of activities or people then the practitioner should make sure they cooperate to make these available.

Some people may require a verbal prompt to begin an activity and another to end the activity if there is not a clear finishing point. It can help to tell them what the next activity is and, if the one that is finishing is a favourite, when it will happen again.

Strategies may involve cues to prepare the person to stop their current activity, to know what the next activity will be and to make the transition between them.

The type of cue used depends on the communication profile of the individual. Often the cue is visual, such as a visual timetable, but it may be verbal or tactile if this is more appropriate for the person.

Cues to prepare the person sometimes involve a countdown to the next activity. This could be an egg timer or stopwatch. Some people may use a verbal countdown or visual cards.

If the learner is engaged in a practical activity, the practitioner should consider how they will know they have completed the task. For example, when breaking up kindling for a fire, make a pile of sticks to be broken and be explicit that the task is complete when all of that pile has been snapped up and put on a new pile.

Some people use visual schedules to show the sequence of activities and to help to show what is happening next, which can help transition. Schedules are often laminated cards with smaller laminated symbols, which can be added and removed as a person makes their way through activities.

People may take cues from the sensory input around them. For instance, being handed a saw may be understood as the cue to begin sawing. This can be a good way to communicate prompts but it is important to remember that once a single meaning is attached to an object or situation then this meaning is likely to become fixed. For example, if the group gathers in a circle for hot chocolate every session and at no other time, the gathering in a circle in that particular place may become a communication that means it's hot chocolate time, and if you then gather everyone in a circle at that place for a different reason then you may have a very aggrieved learner when the expected hot chocolate is not forthcoming!

For some people these strategies may be used throughout their life, while for others they may only be appropriate when they are children. Some people will not need this type of support at all.

How can Forest School be learner led if a particular learner is reliant on prompts to move between activities? The key is to offer choices to the learner whenever possible. Choices should be presented using the communication method which best suits the learner. Too many options may be confusing and in some instances a binary choice may work better. The opportunity to choose is central to empowering people and allowing them to take ownership of their Forest School experience, and the practitioner should ensure that learners have strategies in place to facilitate this.

Usually there is an effort to move away from a reliance on prompts from other people over time, as far as is possible. Forest School should work in partnership with the learner and their supporters to ensure that practice at Forest School is in step with any other support the learner receives.

Intensive interaction

Intensive interaction is a technique using body language and mirroring of a person's actions to connect with autistic people who have limited expressive language and struggle to maintain joint attention.

> Intensive Interaction uses body language to tune into children with whom we find it difficult to communicate. It involves 'learning their language' and responding, not just to 'what' they do but 'how' they do it, since this will tell us how they are feeling. It is more than just copying or mimicking, it means entering their world and working from what it is that their brain finds meaningful.[13]

Intensive interaction approaches can work well in a Forest School setting. The learner-led nature of intensive interaction dovetails nicely into the Forest School approach.

CASE STUDY:
Intensive interaction in a woodland setting

J is a young man who is quite limited in his use of expressive language and communication methods. He very much enjoys the sensory aspects of Forest School. He needs no encouragement to explore the woodland environment and his attention is often centred on the way light and shadow play out through the tree canopy and on the bark of trees. He likes to hold twigs with leaves on them near his face and collects and carries these. He has a favoured spot where he likes to stand and will make different vocal noises while he makes his way through the woods.

One morning, J had made his way to his spot and was standing still intently staring at the textures of the bark on a tall spruce tree. I was preparing some firewood about 20 metres away when J began to whistle short notes. I continued what I was doing but responded to J's whistles by whistling back, at first trying to mimic him but then deliberately trying to change pitch and duration of the note. This naturally developed into a call and response, and after about five minutes J turned and approached me, smiling broadly. J stood over me, looking at me, and continuing to smile and whistle. J then began to press his forehead gently against mine and then to run his forearm along the stubble on my chin. This made J giggle and say 'Mu, mu' (more, more). Our interaction continued over 15 minutes with J smiling and engaged throughout.

Phoebe Caldwell is an expert intensive interaction practitioner who gives these tips:

Empty yourself of your own agenda and enter your partner's world.

Look for what your partner's body language is telling you has meaning for them, the physical feedback they are giving themselves, not just at what they are doing – but how they are doing it, since this will tell you how they are feeling. Watch the whole body rather than just the face.

Tune in to your partner with empathy, using their 'language', with the aim of building up a 'conversation' and emotional engagement. Give them time to respond.

Rather than mimicking and imitating your partner exactly, think of your answer as a response, delivered within their repertoire but with very slight variations to attract their attention.

Look out for negative responses (such as a flinch to light touch), which will indicate hyper or hyposensitivities. Where possible address these.[14]

Stress

Stress has been described as having a major impact on autistic people's ability to function in everyday situations. Heightened stress levels are experienced at all stages of life and can cause significant harm to health and well-being.[15]

Managing stress and anxiety is an important consideration when planning Forest School for an autistic learner. Stress can have a major impact on the ability to interact with the group and on how a person is viewed by others. Stress likes to spread itself around! It makes people behave in ways that make the people around them stressed too. It's important when working with people who may be affected by high levels of stress to be mindful of how others, including yourself, are feeling.

Forest School sessions have the potential to make a positive contribution towards helping someone manage stress and anxiety. The learner-led approach lends itself well to implementing calming strategies. Forest School allows a person the time and space to feel calm if they need to. Demands can be easily reduced and the emphasis on building a relationship with individual learners leads to a higher level of sensitivity to their feelings. The key to helping someone manage stress lies in having the sensitivity to notice it at the outset and help to avoid any escalation. Practitioners are expected to reflect on their own practice and this should lead to an understanding of how the practitioners' own stress can impact on the other people attending sessions. You're just as likely to cause stress to spread as your learners!

Learners can take what they need from sessions and in some cases this may be to use the session itself as a calming strategy. One of the men who comes to my sessions has a particular spot in the woods where he likes to stand, watching the way the light shines through the trees and studying patterns of shadow on fissures in the bark. When stressed he makes his own way to this spot and calms. The only input required from others is to be aware of where he is, that he's safe and to give him the space he needs. At these times this man seems to be experiencing a very direct relationship with the woods with a clear benefit in terms of his well-being. This is the relationship with place that was discussed in Chapter 4. By recognising the importance of this relationship, and allowing the learner to seek and develop this on their own terms, Forest School has allowed this man to develop his own calming strategy and to teach it to the practitioner and other supporters. We can see the benefit of allowing the learner to lead and how this would contrast with an approach that attempted to hold his attention on an activity from which he was gaining nothing at that moment, and which would probably exacerbate his stress.

As part of pre-session preparation the practitioner should consider how best to work in partnership with the learner, and any others who are attending the session with them, in order to help them avoid unnecessary stress during the session and to ensure that they are aware of any calming strategies that the learner uses.

A great deal of stress is often caused by others, whether through deliberate actions or a general lack of awareness, and it's these triggers that you can learn to avoid. This is an important part of the process of building a trusting relationship between learner, practitioner and place, which was described in Chapter 4.

The practitioner should learn the early indicators of stress in an individual's behaviour. For some this may be a facial expression, phrase or increased repetitive physical movements ('stimming'). For others this may present as thinking becoming more inflexible and conversation becoming more repetitive. Often the initial signs may be quite subtle. One of the men who attends my session scratches his head when he begins to feel stressed.

At this point, you have an opportunity to help the learner to reduce their stress level. Sometimes this simply involves giving them the space to use their own calming strategies. It's important that you recognise what these are. Learning these strategies is an important part of building a relationship with the learner.

The first thing to consider if a learner is showing signs that they may become stressed is whether you are the best person to help them to calm. Be realistic about your competency. If there is someone else present who is more familiar to the learner and whom they trust and communicate well with, then the best advice to the Forest School practitioner is to discreetly make sure this person is aware of the situation and to give them the space to help the learner.

Remember that phrase 'too much information'? Bear this in mind if someone is becoming stressed. Autistic people often describe this build up of stress as feeling overwhelmed with information coming in at a faster rate than they can process. Most calming strategies rely on reducing this input:

- Reduce demands.

- Keep attempts at communication simple. It is better that only one supporter attempts communication.

- Consider the most effective way to communicate:

  One system may be taught as a primary means of communication (for instance, speech or signs) and a different system may be used to repair communicative breakdowns (for example, gestures, a picture system). (Wetherby and Prizant 1992)[16]

  Visual methods of communication are sometimes more effective at these times as many autistic people find information easier to process if it is presented visually. Some other people may seek reassurance by going through a repetitive verbal interaction. As always, the key is knowledge of the learner as an individual.

- If you can identify triggers then, if possible, remove or resolve them.

- Plan ahead. Would the learner like to have a quiet space available to move into when stressed? If possible, identify this by directly involving the learner in choosing a space or by observing the learner to see if they have a favoured area which seems to calm them. Some learners may seek calm areas where they feel enclosed, such as a den or sensory hammock. Some may want to experience a sensory stimulus such as rocking. Would the learner like to have anything available in this area? Make sure that creating this space is part of the programme in initial sessions.

A very useful tip I was given at the beginning of my career, when responding to autistic people who have good verbal communication, is to verbally acknowledge their feelings if they are becoming stressed. In neurotypical interactions, people can pick up on empathetic body language that is acknowledging their emotions; this empathetic acknowledgement helps to reassure someone that their feelings are being taken seriously and will be addressed. Without picking up on this body language, autistic people may feel that they need to escalate their behaviour until they get a response that they recognise. Simply by saying, 'I see that you are sad/angry/upset...' you can remove the perceived need to escalate behaviour so that feelings are acknowledged.

When helping someone to calm remember the saying 'less is more'. You are trying to reduce and simplify any input which the person is not seeking themselves. The better you learn to respond to initial indicators of stress, the less likely it is that you will have to deal with the more extreme behaviours that stress can cause.

Demand avoidance and 'getting stuck'

Some interactions encountered by the practitioner during sessions can be frustrating if they are not properly understood as symptoms of stress or anxiety.

The two most common in my experience are 'getting stuck' and demand avoidance. 'Getting stuck' describes a situation where the autistic person cannot move on from a particular action. This may be physical, with the person sometimes freezing altogether, or it may be an inability to move on from a particular question or statement in an interaction. Getting stuck is often the result of having too much to process, which may have been caused by underlying stress. It's important that the practitioner recognises that this may be an indicator of stress and responds accordingly. Use the advice given above to reduce demand and attempt to communicate in a manner that is easier to understand. Sometimes a change of face can help someone to move on, and it may be worth allowing another supporter to take over the interaction, particularly if they have a good relationship with the learner.

Demand avoidant behaviours are another symptom of underlying stress. Different people may present different types of demand avoidance depending on their communication profile. People who have no spoken language and are limited in their use of communication systems sometimes express themselves using behaviours such as biting their hand to refuse perceived demands.

Some people who are more able communicators may develop social strategies to avoid demands such as making excuses, distracting the person making the demand or ignoring them altogether.

If an autistic learner is presenting demand avoidant behaviour this often indicates underlying stress or confusion. Recognise this and don't get drawn into an unnecessary battle of wills. Reflect on your own approach. Are you communicating in the best way? Has the learner been properly prepared to transition from what they are doing to the next activity? Are there any obvious stressors that you can remove from the interaction? Is this the best time to make the communication? Remember that this behaviour may be an indication that the learner is starting to feel overwhelmed by processing differences.

As always, making the right call in this situation depends on knowledge of the learner as a person and having a trusting and mutually respectful relationship. Sometimes this behaviour is just a way to buy some extra time to process what is happening before responding, and the practitioner can reflect on this and adjust their communication as necessary.

All of us present demand avoidant behaviours to some extent – just ask my partner about the many and varied ruses I employ to escape DIY jobs! However, for some people the avoidance of demands placed on them can become extreme and ultimately can cause them significant problems. Pathological demand avoidance (PDA) is a profile that describes the extremes of this behaviour. PDA is not universally recognised but is gaining increasing acceptance among professionals.[17] It is believed that the underlying cause of PDA is anxiety and people with this profile will go to great lengths to resist demands being placed on them. If other strategies fail they may resort to challenging behaviour that seems out of proportion to the situation. Supporting PDA requires strategies that may seem counter-intuitive compared with those used with other autistic people. If you are consistently observing extremes of demand avoidant behaviour it may be worth exploring the possibility of a PDA profile with other supporters and seeking advice on how to develop approaches that will better serve the learner.

Conclusion

The social aspect of Forest School should not put off either autistic people and their supporters or practitioners who are considering running autism-inclusive sessions. We've discussed how the Forest School approach can provide time and space for all learners and how the Forest School pedagogy encourages all participants to engage on their own terms and to be valued for who they are. Autism-inclusive Forest School should seek to create a nurturing social environment in which all learners can develop as equals and, most importantly, have fun in the way that suits them best.

KEY POINTS

▸ Whatever the size of the group, Forest School will involve social interaction and this is an area in which autistic learners may require support and understanding.

▸ If a practitioner is autism aware then a learner-led approach has the potential to allow an autistic learner to engage with the group on their own terms.

▶ For many autistic people, clear roles and rules make social situations easier to navigate but they may be inflexible in how they interpret these.

▶ There are differences in the ways in which autistic children play, particularly around the social and symbolic aspects of play. Research shows that early social play interventions can help children to learn how to better interact with others later in life, and practitioners should work in partnership with learners and supporters to carry any interventions of this nature over into Forest School. However, practitioners should not lose sight of the ways in which autistic children like to play naturally and it is important to recognise that autistic play is an equally valid way to learn about the world.

▶ Some autistic learners may require prompts to initiate actions or support transitions between different activities. These should be carried out using any systems that the learner and their supporters already have in place.

▶ People who present higher levels of impairment when interacting with others can establish social connections if the practitioner learns how to enter their world with understanding and with an open attitude to learning about that person on their terms. A very valuable technique that relates to this is intensive interaction.

▶ Stress has a major impact on the lives of many autistic people and how they interact with others. Managing stress is a key aspect of working with autistic people. An empathetic outlook is vital. Avoiding triggering unnecessary stress, and recognising initial signs of stress then de-escalating as early as possible are skills that practitioners should seek to develop. An understanding of the learner as an individual and establishing a relationship built on trust and respect are ideas central to Forest School pedagogy and this approach provides a solid foundation on which the practitioner can support the learner to manage stress.

CHAPTER 7

Forest School and the Sensory Environment

In earlier chapters, we touched on the differences in sensory processing experienced by many autistic people. Research suggests that at least 70 per cent of autistic people experience differences in sensory processing.[1]

DSM-5 includes differences in sensory sensitivity in the diagnostic criteria for ASD and this reflects the development of better understanding of this aspect of autistic experience. Research in this area has, to some extent, been prompted by the anecdotal evidence provided by autistic people themselves and their supporters.

For some people, these differences may only affect them some of the time, but for others they may have a profound impact on how that person perceives the world and functions within it. Differences in sensory processing can underlie many of the outward signs of autism, and developing an awareness of a person's sensory needs is an important part of supporting and empowering them.

We all experience the world around us through our seven senses:

- Sight: our eyes sense the light, colour, movement and forms in our environment.

- Hearing: our ears sense the sounds around us, their volume, tone and pitch.

- Touch: our skin gives us tactile sensitivity and allows us to perceive texture, form and density.

- Smell: our noses sense the smells in our environment. We make strong judgements based on our sense of smell. Some smells may attract us, others may be repellent.

- Taste: our sense of taste is connected to our sense of smell and helps us to assess the food we eat. The mouth is a very sensitive organ. Our lips and tongues are very tactile and we can judge consistency using proprioceptive sense from our teeth and jaws. As babies, we use our mouths to explore everything but as we grow this is discouraged. There are strong taboos around how we use our mouths to explore the world and these are connected to ideas about keeping germs from entering our bodies via our mouths and also from the sexual dimension of oral contact with other people.

- Proprioception: our joints and muscles sense where we are in the world. Feelings of pressure, tension and position help us to perceive where we are in space and make us aware of our bodies in relation to the surrounding environment.

- Vestibular: our inner ear provides our sense of balance. Balance is essential to help us to move our bodies through the environment.

We also have senses that register pain and temperature. We rely on our senses to experience the environment around us in any given moment and the way our senses work is integral to how we come to understand the world.

How keenly our senses work varies from one person to another and this changes throughout our lives and can be affected in the short term by factors such as illness, fatigue, stress or intoxicants. However, some people experience sensory processing that lies outside the typical range and impacts on their ability to function. This is described as sensory processing disorder (SPD) and is common in people with an ASD, although by no means restricted to them.

If you have read this book from the beginning you will probably guess what is coming next. As with pretty much every aspect of autism, the exact way in which sensory differences affect an individual varies a great deal from one person to the next. For some people, sensory differences may only require a couple of simple accommodations or strategies to nullify any negative impact they have on that person's life, but for other people their sensory processing differences are potentially the most disabling aspect of their autism.

Hypo- and hypersensitivity

Autistic people may experience hypo- (under) or hyper- (over) sensitivity to sensory stimuli. Hypersensitivity means that too much sensory information is being relayed to the brain. This makes sensory experiences very intense, sometimes unbearably so, and when people experience this they can become overwhelmed and find it impossible to focus on anything else. The practitioner should reflect on times in their own life when they have been exposed to intense sensory stimuli – road drills outside your house when you have a headache, blinding direct sunlight when trying to drive or intensely foul smells. These types of experience provoke a visceral reaction and you have to understand that an autistic person who is experiencing sensory hypersensitivity may be having this kind of experience and quite possibly to a level of intensity that you would struggle to imagine.

Hyposensitivity means that the senses aren't relaying enough information to the brain and the person may need to seek additional sensory input to compensate. This can lead to sensory-seeking behaviours that can appear odd to others, such as banging objects, rocking the body or tasting things with strong or bitter flavours that most people would find unpleasant. People may also find it hard to judge where their body is in space and to perceive depth. Everyday actions such as stepping from a kerb can become very challenging. People moving into your space can seem frightening if your senses make it seem as if they are rushing towards you.

Hypersensitivity can cause unpleasant, or even painful, experiences, but it can also cause very pleasurable experiences. The person can become completely engrossed in the sensory experience, for instance sunlight falling through the leaf canopy or the feeling of movement when they rock their body. Earlier in the book I suggested that the reader watched the film *Too Much Information* on YouTube. This film shows a boy experiencing hypersensitivity in a shopping mall to the point of sensory overload. However, I would also ask the reader to watch Amanda Baggs's *In My Language* on YouTube. This inspirational film shows another side to autistic sensory experience.

Levels of hypo- or hypersensitivity can fluctuate depending on how a person feels and how they are processing information at that moment. Strategies and accommodations are put in place to help people to regulate their senses when they need to. People who find high-pitched sounds intolerable may be supplied with ear plugs or headphones; people who are sensitive to light may be given glasses with coloured lenses or people may choose clothes which are made from fabrics that don't irritate sensitive skin. Whenever possible, people should be given prior warning of any sensory stimuli that they won't like and adaptations may be made to environments they use regularly. Most autistic people develop their own self-regulatory sensory strategies and these are referred to as 'stimming'.

Stimming

'Stimming' is the word used to describe self-stimulatory behaviours. These are repetitive actions such as movements, sounds or phrases which are often carried out by autistic people. Stimming takes lots of different forms depending on the individual and which sense they are trying to stimulate. Obvious examples would include rocking, hand flapping or spinning objects but there really are a lot of ways to stim! Autistic people stim for different reasons. Sometimes it may be a way to self-regulate hyper- or hyposensitivity, sometimes it may calm anxiety and may indicate that a person is feeling stressed, but sometimes it probably just feels too damn good not to!

Some stimming may be done to an extreme which actually causes injury to the person, often through hand biting or banging the head against surfaces, and in these cases strategies must be put in place to lessen harm, such as offering a sensory toy which is made to be bitten on.

When considering autistic stimming we need to be aware that we all stim to some extent. Drumming your fingers on a table, whistling a tune to yourself, playing with your hair – this is all stimming, but neurotypical people usually restrict their stimming techniques to methods deemed socially acceptable. Autistic stimming can manifest in ways which neurotypicals find hard to relate to and in settings where it is not considered appropriate.

From the perspective of a Forest School practitioner, stimming is a great thing (as long as it carries no risk of harm). Stimming will communicate how someone is feeling and will teach you what stimuli that person seeks above others. This information is vital to understanding what type of activities that person may be most likely to engage in and how to present an activity to them. For example, if you have observed someone seeking tactile stimuli – perhaps picking up small twigs or brash and gently rolling them in the hand whenever they can – then you can incorporate this into the leaf-rubbing activity, described in Chapter 10, by encouraging the person to feel each leaf and its different textures and shapes. We will discuss activities that can provide different stimuli later in this chapter.

Stimming can be the key to achieving a genuinely learner-led approach with autistic people. In the last chapter, we discussed how some autistic learners may require prompts to initiate action. Stimming is almost always learner led and self-initiated. People who seek stimuli and explore the sensory environment are taking ownership of their Forest School experience and this should be recognised and, as long as it's safe, encouraged.

Sensory overload

Sometimes autistic people may experience sensory overload. Sensory overload is when one or more senses are receiving sensory information at a faster rate, or intensity, than they can manage to process.

The *Too Much Information* film mentioned earlier tries to give the viewer an insight into what this may feel like. Remember that the feelings are overwhelming and make someone feel as if they are being assaulted and have lost control of what is happening to them. As well as being scared, they may be experiencing pain and discomfort.

Trying to avoid this kind of experience is very important. Different people may have different strategies they can use. These may involve blocking the sense out, for example using ear plugs, or stimming to distract from one sense by increasing the stimulation in another.

People may develop involuntary strategies such as automatically beginning to process through only one sensory channel – this is the 'monoprocessing' mentioned in Chapter 5 – or their brain may temporarily stop attaching meaning to the information their senses are sending it. This is called sensory agnosia. Someone may still perceive the objects around them but cannot interpret what they are. This can be a very frightening experience.

Some people may learn to experience a sense peripherally. This means the person will avoid direct perception as this may bring too much stimuli to process. For example, the person may find it difficult to look directly at someone's face when listening to what they say because they find it hard to process the words spoken and the movement of the face simultaneously.

When trying to support someone experiencing sensory overload it is important to follow the same advice which was offered in the last chapter when we discussed stress. A trusted person should offer support, while trying to keep interaction to the minimum necessary, and stimuli should be removed or reduced, preferably by ensuring that a quiet and safe space is available.

There are different ways to provide a space for people to retreat to when they feel overloaded and establishing if this is required and working out how to provide it is an important part of preparation. Bear in mind that if a sensory channel is being overloaded you need to provide the person with the opportunity to reduce the stimuli coming from that channel. Strategies to reduce sensory input need the same consideration as activities that can provide stimuli. Sometimes the person may have their own strategies in place and you should consider how these can be accommodated in your session.

Different perceptions

As well as experiencing sensory stimuli at different levels of intensity, autistic people may be processing sensory information in a different way.

Gestalt perception is the term used to describe a tendency to experience everything as a whole, rather than as a combination of different items. Neurotypical people usually have an automatic editor which filters sensory information as it is received and decides what needs to be focused on and what can be relegated to the background. Autistic people tend not to do this automatically and so find it hard to filter the sensory information they receive into separate items that combine to make a coherent whole. For example, it may be hard to focus on part of a picture that is being held up by someone – the person may see the individual holding the picture, the ground, the sky, everything, as one and find it very difficult to deliberately focus on one detail. In Chapter 5, I briefly mentioned the difficulty that some autistic people have in filtering out background noise and concentrating on the voice of someone who is speaking to them. This is another example of gestalt perception, with the auditory environment being perceived as a whole.

This ties in with weak central coherence, mentioned in Chapter 2. If someone is experiencing everything as a whole, rather than as foreground and background, a small change in detail will completely change the entire scene and it will all become a new whole. This type of perception is therefore much more sensitive to small changes of detail which typical perception relegates to the background and overlooks. It's important to recognise that this way of experiencing the world is often a strength rather than an impairment. A good example of this is the ability that autistic people often have to see through conjuring tricks. A magician relies on diverting the audience's attention away from their sleight of hand during a trick. By exploiting the tendency to focus on foreground details, and be less aware of the background, the conjuror can fool their audience. However, the autistic onlooker perceives the whole scene with equal focus and is less easily distracted from the sleight of hand.

Some autistic people may develop fragmented processing. This happens to help someone cope with having more information to process than the brain can manage. Fragmented processing means that the person is experiencing stimuli as separate units of information, picked out from the whole but experienced as separate and singular. Without the efficient internal 'editor' that neurotypical people have, the bigger picture and the detail aren't being experienced together. For example, when looking at someone's face, the person may see a nostril, then an earlobe, then movement of lips but at no point perceive these things as part of a coherent, interconnected face. It is no wonder that someone perceiving the world like this may struggle to interpret body language.

Some autistic people describe distortions in their perception, which take different forms. Synaesthesia is when stimuli received through one sense is processed by a different sense, for example hearing a particular noise is experienced as a distinct taste. Sometimes people may experience changes in the shape or size of objects, or space seeming to expand or contract. These experiences may be hard to relate to but the practitioner should understand that they are very real sensations for the people who experience them.

How can Forest School benefit someone with differences in sensory processing?

In Chapter 4, we discussed the importance of place in the Forest School approach. Forest School centres on experiential learning and our experience of place comes, in its purest form, through our senses. If your senses are experiencing things more intensely, you become very aware of place, because the sensory stimuli in that environment are either causing you discomfort or fascinating you. Equally, if you are trying to balance under-sensitivity by seeking sensation to ground yourself, then what stimuli are available (and the opportunity to seek them) becomes very important.

Public spaces, primarily designed for neurotypical people, can be quite hostile environments for someone with a sensory processing disorder – noisy and busy and often with different things deliberately competing for our attention. There may be unpleasant sensory stimuli such as high-pitched sounds, strong smells or people staring, and these can crop up suddenly and with no warning. At the same time, there are social expectations of how someone can behave, so stimming can draw disapproving looks and there are strict taboos surrounding which senses you can use to explore the environment. A journey through this kind of environment may need careful planning and suitable safety gear, such as ear plugs or tinted glasses.

Some spaces are designed primarily for autistic people. Sometimes these may be completely individualised, such as someone's home, making sure that stimuli that the person is averse to aren't present and stimuli that they need to seek are. Sometimes a place may be designed to be used by groups of autistic people, with varying sensory profiles, and so is more of a generalised environment with lighting, sounds and so on kept to a low level and space and equipment provided for different sensory needs.

Sometimes there is a specific sensory room, or 'snoezelen', available for people to use. These rooms contain different sensory experiences which the person can choose – these often involve softly shifting light, gentle sounds such as recorded birdsong, and different textures to touch. When sitting in a sensory room it's hard not to be struck by how many of these experiences can be found in the woods – light shifting as clouds pass and the tree canopy moves in the breeze, the sound of real birdsong or gentle rain on a tarpaulin shelter, and the different textures of rough bark, soft leaves or smooth stone.

I would argue that wild natural spaces don't favour one type of sensory processing over another. They are rich sensory environments, but generally the intensity of stimuli is lower than in many neurotypical environments. Wild environments cannot be controlled to the extent that places designed especially for autism can be. There could be unwanted stimuli such as buzzing insects, thunder or the feel of rain on the skin, but these can often be anticipated beforehand and planned for. The slower pace of nature, together with the extra physical space and the space in time intrinsic to the Forest School approach, can contribute to a gentler sensory experience than that offered by many shared public spaces.

Wild places aren't primarily human spaces. They contain all kinds of life – animals, plants, bugs and birds – all existing in different ways yet sharing the same environment. Diversity is inherent in wild places. People relate to nature in very different ways depending on their individual perspective and the culture to which they belong. Autistic experiences of wild places are as valid as any other. The autistic person's sensory relationship with place, a central tenet of Forest School for all learners, can be experienced and expressed on their terms; the practitioner's role is to observe, collect evidence and try to learn from the interactions between learner and place that they witness.

Sensory observation

The learner-led approach of Forest School, taking place in a natural sensory environment, is a great way to gather evidence which can contribute to a sensory profile for the learner. Sensory profiles are assessment instruments, in the form of checklists or questionnaires, completed by the person and their supporters, and can be used to contribute to diagnosis and to assess which stimuli a learner seeks or avoids. They are helpful for planning strategies and accommodations to mitigate the impact that sensory processing differences have on the person's life.

Different interventions may be put in place to help people to cope with differences in sensory processing. Sensory integration therapy seeks to desensitise people to sensations which may cause problems through hypersensitivity and to provide stimuli that are lacking due to hyposensitivity. Occupational therapists may create an individual sensory diet for someone. This provides the sensory input a person requires to maintain a feeling of well-being. If the learner is taking part in these types of programmes then it is important that the practitioner tries to work in partnership with other supporters to incorporate these approaches into Forest School.

As well as contributing to sensory interventions, observations of which sensory channels people prefer to use to engage with the world around them can contribute to developing more effective communication with autistic learners. By identifying which senses the learner favours, the practitioner can establish which methods of communication will be more meaningful for them.

Sensory observations are important when planning Forest School sessions. The practitioner can engage learners in new activities by ensuring that there is a sensory aspect to the activity which is known to interest the learner. Equally you can plan activities that give the learner the opportunity to avoid stimuli they do not like.

Making sensory observations is straightforward and involves recording what you see in a simple, factual manner. The practitioner does not need to be an expert in sensory processing, or necessarily understand exactly what their observations may indicate – what is important is that a record is kept, which can be shared with other people involved with the individual's support and which details what has been observed.

All activities are sensory activities. The practitioner should try to develop an awareness of how an activity is likely to be experienced by the learner. This will involve getting in touch with your own senses and consciously paying attention to the details of sensory experience which you may normally overlook. Imagine taking a leaf between your fingers. What does it feel like? Soft? Smooth? Can you feel the veins that run through it, or its shape? How firm is it when pressure is applied? Does it smell? What does it look like when held to the light? What does it look like when it moves in different ways – does the shape change when it is in motion? Consider how the information about the leaf is perceived across your different senses. Learning to empathise with people who are experiencing differences in sensory perception begins with becoming aware of your own senses and how they connect you to the world. As this happens, you should begin to feel a deeper connection to place and an awareness of the woods around you.

Always remember when offering a new sensory activity that it may be uncomfortable, scary or even painful for the learner. Under no circumstances should a learner be encouraged to continue with an activity if there is any indication at all that it is causing them stress or discomfort. Allow learners to lead you and to engage at their own pace, or to refuse altogether. There is no rush, and a refusal can teach the practitioner far more about the learner than pressing someone to do something they are not comfortable with.

Remember that differences in sensory processing aren't necessarily impairments:

> Autistic individuals with their heightened senses often can appreciate colours, smells, tastes to a much higher degree than people around them. Their gifts and talents should be nurtured.[2]

I find that when I observe a learner seeking particular sensory stimuli, the best way to gain an insight into what they may be experiencing is to copy what I am observing. Only by following the learner's lead and lying back and looking up do I notice the amazing way that woodsmoke drifts and curls through beams of sunlight cutting through the leaf canopy and I need to close my eyes and run my fingertips across the bark of a tree trunk to begin to understand what the learner may be experiencing when they do the same.

Below I give some examples of sensory observations I have made in my sessions and in activities I have offered. This is by no means exhaustive but I hope it will give the practitioner the basic idea of how to incorporate an awareness of sensory needs into their practice.

Sight
Sensory observations

- Being distracted by light or movement. The person may enjoy sitting quietly watching the flames of a fire, or lying back watching the light shine through the overhead leaf canopy. They might enjoy spinning objects and then watching them or be fascinated by shiny surfaces.

- Indications that a person is trying to reduce stimuli include holding hands close to the eyes, standing very close and focusing on a close-up of an object, for example the trunk of a tree, or avoiding looking directly at things such as faces, fires or sunlight.

Sensory activities

- Play Forest School bingo (Chapter 10).

- Have a fire (Chapter 10).

- Encourage the whole group to lie back and watch the way the light shines through the overhead leaf canopy.

- Do some photography. It is good practice to take photographs to evidence the work you are doing (with consent in place to do so). Encourage the learners to use the camera, if this interests them.

- Use magnifying glasses to explore the surroundings.

- For people who seek to reduce stimuli, offer activities that provide enclosure – sitting inside dens and tents or wrapped up in a hammock with the face covered.

Sound
Sensory observations

- Making noises, banging objects or enjoying music.

- Feeling stressed by unexpected or high-pitched noises, or having difficulty picking out one noise from others.

Sensory activities

- Incorporate music into sessions, either singing or making improvised instruments from things found in the forest – look for things to bang together, rattle or whistle into.

- Draw soundscapes – the learner sits listening and when they hear a noise they draw the noise in colour on a sheet of paper. The learner chooses where to draw the noise in relation to how far away they think it came from. The learner chooses the colour and shape they think represents the noise. This can be quite a difficult concept for some autistic learners to grasp and the practitioner needs to consider if they can communicate how to do this activity.

- Have a quiet space available where learners can be still and hear the woods. Birdsong, the breeze, rain on a tarpaulin shelter – the woods are full of sounds.

- Reflect on how the practitioner can introduce sound to activities. For example, using a bowsaw could be accompanied by saying, 'One and two and three and four...' in time with the rhythm of the sawing.

- Learn verbal routines, word play or call and response noises that individual learners enjoy and incorporate these into the session. One of the men who comes to my sessions only enjoys taking part in tasks using tools with me if I repeat his favourite phrases while we work together.

- Consider how to reduce noise if the person is overloaded. Some people may use ear defenders but don't lose sight of one of Forest School's greatest assets – space. Learners who are finding particular noises overwhelming, such as another learner being noisy, can be offered an activity away from the source of the noise.

Smell
Sensory observations

- Choosing to hold objects up and sniff them on their own initiative.

- Choosing to sit deliberately near smells such as woodsmoke, even going so far as moving to be nearer to the smoke if it changes direction.

- Noticeably avoiding smells that other people easily tolerate.

Sensory activities

- Encourage the use of smell by the whole group. For example:

  - When sawing green wood, encourage the group to sniff the freshly cut piece of wood. Different woods have distinctly different smells. I may be showing my age here, but do you remember the Pepsi® Challenge? Try a Forest School version. Get the learner to smell the different types of wood while you name them and then ask them to close their eyes and try to identify the pieces of cut wood by smell alone.

– Try the charcoal-making activity described in Chapter 10. Get the group to touch and smell the cut pieces of wood before and after the charcoal-making process.

– If you have a rain shower, encourage the group to close their eyes and smell the air. Have you heard the word 'petrichor'? What a great word! It describes the smell of fresh rain falling on dry soil.

• When you cook or make a hot drink, consider the smells the food will make when being prepared and cooked. Will the learner want to seek or avoid the smells of different types of food?

• Be sensitive to the need of some learners to avoid certain smells and make sure that they are not expected to take part in an activity that will be unpleasant for them to experience. Remember to promote inclusivity by having different choices of activity which people can choose to take part in and also by realising that some people may prefer to watch from a safe distance.

Taste

Taste is one sense that can cause problems in natural settings. This will be discussed in Chapter 8.

Sensory observations

• Using taste to explore natural environments – lifting objects up to taste with the tongue or licking objects. Is taste alone being used or is the person biting on the object to perceive its density or using their lips and tongue to explore texture?

Are they trying to eat the object or using their mouth to explore it before spitting it out?

- Cravings for, or aversion to, certain foods. Is this related to taste or texture or density? Is it generalised across foodstuffs with similar tastes, textures and density? Does the learner prefer very bland food or do they seek strong flavours?

Sensory activities

- The practitioner will need to give careful consideration to how they can incorporate taste into sessions in a safe manner. Preparing food and drink is the most obvious way to provide these stimuli safely. When considering what type of food to introduce to the learner during sessions you need to take into account their personal preferences and any dietary considerations (such as food intolerance and religious or cultural preferences). Remember again that inclusivity is achieved through offering appropriate choices to the whole group that take everyone's needs into account. In my experience, cooking outdoors sometimes encourages people to try foods they do not usually eat in other settings but any new foods should be offered as a choice, which the learner has control over and does not feel pressured to try.

Touch
Sensory observations

- Seeking touch. This can be quite subtle. Learners may be seen to pick up small objects such as little twigs and hold them in their hands or run them between their fingers. When they are handed something, they may be observed to run their fingers along the object, feeling its texture and shape. They may hold things in their hands when they aren't engaged in an activity or rub their fingertips together or along clothes or objects in the immediate vicinity. These actions can be difficult to notice if you aren't looking for them. Often the learner doesn't look at whatever they are touching, and neurotypical people tend to follow a person's gaze when trying to perceive where that person's attention is directed.

- Avoiding certain textures and showing an adverse reaction if they come into contact with them. They may choose to wear safety gloves when they aren't required or refuse to wear them when they are.

- Finding it uncomfortable to wear weather-appropriate clothing and needing to try different types of weatherproof clothing to find garments that feel right. They may prefer to use an umbrella rather than wear a hat or pull a hood over their head.

- Disliking being touched unexpectedly. They may be sensitive to light touch but be better able to cope with deeper touch.

Sensory activities

- Be aware of the tactile aspect of an activity. For instance, if going on a walk where you are identifying different types of tree then encourage the group to touch the bark and leaves and feel the different shapes and textures of different trees.

- Try a touch version of the Pepsi® Challenge. Collect objects during a walk then see if the learners can identify them by touch alone.

- Make worry beads from elder. Elder grows wild throughout the UK and is familiar to people for its clusters of elderberries and elderflowers. Elder has a lot of old superstitions surrounding it, notably that burning it brings death into the house, although elder growing outside the house is said to keep the devil away. Young branches have a soft pith running through their centre and can be used to make beads quite easily. Use loppers to cut the branches off the plant (superstitious people will need to ask the permission of the Lady of the Woods first!). Once you have your branch, use a hacksaw to cut your beads to size and a metal tent peg to poke the soft pith out of the centre. You can peel the bark off altogether, peel parts of it off to make stripes on the bead or leave it on. Repeat until you have a few beads to thread onto string. You can add other found objects to the string if you like and can even cut medallions of different types of wood from a branch using a bowsaw before making a hole to thread the string through with a hand drill. The ends of the string are tied together and the beads can be worn as a necklace or carried and run through the hands like worry beads.

- Some people may really like feeling soft, wet textures. Muddy play provides the chance to seek this type of stimuli but make sure that there is water and soap so that hands can be washed afterwards. Making dough gives similar feelings and can be rolled into chapatis to be cooked over the fire. Another way to offer these stimuli is working with clay-making faces on trees or small animals and figurines from the clay and found objects.

- Some people may seek to avoid certain tactile stimuli and may need to have gloves available to help them to do so.

Vestibular
Sensory observations

- Stimming by rocking or spinning the body.

- Being very focused on movement in play – balancing on logs, swinging on branches and so on.

- Avoiding lots of movement in play or seeming to feel uncomfortable if both feet are off the ground simultaneously.

- Having difficulty walking on uneven ground.

Sensory activities

- Set up a rope swing – a good way to provide vestibular stimuli. London Play has produced an excellent guide which fully explains how to safely set up a tree swing. It can be downloaded for free from: http://fairplayforchildren.org/ pdf/1289571512.pdf.

- Put up a hammock between two trees. Hammocks can be bought cheaply and are a great way to bring that rocking motion into your sessions. I use hammocks that are designed for camping out and have a zip running the length of the hammock which allows you to zip yourself inside. This is a great way to lessen visual stimuli or to provide a feeling of enclosure for people who like this.

- Make a mud slides as a fun way to gain vestibular sensations but make sure that learners have waterproofs on and don't get too cold.

- Use a bowsaw to provide a gently rhythmic rocking motion.

- Be aware that some people find vestibular activities very unpleasant, so do not pressure anyone to take part in swinging games who does not wish to do so. Make sure that alternatives of equal interest are available.

Proprioception
Sensory observations

- Holding their body in unusual positions which appear to stress joints and muscles.

- Having difficulty in judging where the body is in space, for example seeming to have difficulty in sitting down in a smooth motion or walking along paths when there is light foliage overgrowing, and seeming to find it hard to judge where to put the feet, resulting in hesitant motion.

- Seeking deep pressure – often asking for hugs, pressing themselves against surfaces, initiating rough-and-tumble play a lot.

- Having difficulty in judging how hard to press a tool or crayon, either pressing down too hard or using too light a touch.

Sensory activities

- Use hammocks to provide deep pressure. The body's weight produces the pressure and, if desired, this can be increased by pulling the hammock material tightly around the person lying in it.

- Carry heavy things to provide proprioceptive stimuli – particularly rucksacks when there is enough weight to transmit pressure through the shoulder straps.

- Try tree climbing, particularly hanging from branches.

- Hug a tree – this will stimulate proprioception but runs the risk of making people think that you're a hippy! Good fun though, if you're willing to take that chance.

Remember that the level of sensitivity can fluctuate and do not assume that because a learner has responded in a particular way on one occasion, they will always react in the same way. Offer choices, without pressure, and watch for patterns emerging over time.

I feel that reflecting on how to better understand the sensory needs of autistic learners has made my own perception of the woods deeper and richer and I consider this to be one of the great lessons my learners have taught me.

KEY POINTS

- The majority of autistic people experience differences in sensory processing.

- These differences are individual. A sensory experience which one autistic person may actively seek may be very unpleasant for someone else.

- Developing an awareness of sensory needs can help someone to develop accommodations that enable them to cope better in day-to-day life and empower them to reach their potential.

- Forest School provides a rich sensory environment and learner-led approaches give participants the opportunity to seek, or avoid, sensory experiences.

- Activities can be planned around an individual's sensory preferences and this approach is likely to lead to better engagement from the participant and can help them to regulate their sensory input.

- The practitioner should aim to work in partnership with other supporters to establish a sensory profile for the participant and seek to carry any interventions, such as sensory diets, over into Forest School sessions. The practitioner should also seek to increase their personal awareness of the sensory environment and make observations of how their learners interact with their surroundings.

- Understand that sensory differences are not necessarily impairments but can be strengths if they are considered when planning sessions.

CHAPTER 8

Staying Safe

One of the causes of 'nature deficit disorder' identified by Richard Louv[1] is the fear that many parents have of allowing their children to play in natural settings. This type of risk aversion is increasingly recognised as creating its own hazard, namely hampering the social and physical development of the children concerned.

Risk aversion can lead to equally bad outcomes for people with a perceived disability. For some disabled people, the risk-adverse attitudes held by those who support them can be more disabling than their actual impairments. This is recognised in the guidance for best practice in the UK, which encourages an approach that recognises that an element of risk underpins the right of an individual to make choices and control their own life.

The Forest School approach encourages a 'safe enough' attitude, which recognises the benefits of risk but also the need to ensure that any exposure to risk is thought through beforehand and carefully managed. In earlier chapters, we discussed the importance of building trust between the learner, practitioner and place and the sensitive management of risk is an important part of building this trust. The learner must learn to trust the practitioner not to put them into situations in which they may be harmed, and the practitioner must learn to trust that the learner will not behave in ways which may cause harm to themselves, others or the environment.

Equally importantly, the practitioner must gain the trust of the learner's supporters. They have to feel positive that the learner is in safe hands. The practitioner needs to adopt a sensitive approach with supporters. Be aware of the fact that that risk-adverse attitudes towards the learner may have originated from stressful experiences in the past. Gaining trust can be a slow process and, again, we can see how the space in time inherent in Forest School can lend itself well to meeting the needs of autistic learners.

In order to gain trust, the practitioner must be able to show an awareness of safety and to have robust procedures in place to ensure that any risk to learners is minimised.

There are four main areas the practitioner needs to consider:

- The environment the sessions take place in.

- The weather.

- The activity itself.

- The individual taking part.

Risk assessments

Any aspect of Forest School which has the potential to carry any chance of harm to the participants should be subject to prior risk assessment. Risk assessments are documents produced to demonstrate that thought has been given to any potential hazard and reasonable steps have been taken to minimise the likelihood of harm occurring.

The risk-assessment process is covered in Forest School training and anyone already supporting autistic people in different settings should already be aware of it. Documents come in different formats, but all identify what the potential hazard is, the likelihood of it occurring, and measures which can be put in place to reduce the risk of harm. Risk assessment is an ongoing process and should be reviewed whenever there is a change in any of the factors assessed or after a stated period if all factors remain the same.

It's important that risk assessment is viewed as a positive process. The point of a risk assessment should be to give the learners the opportunity to do things and it shouldn't be used as an instrument to deny people activities that they will benefit from. Robust risk assessments prove that the safety of participants has been properly considered and demonstrate the safety awareness which should reassure a learner's supporters.

Emergency procedure

Forest School practitioners are required to have a qualification in outdoor first aid and to have an emergency procedure in place.

An emergency procedure should give details of how to respond to minor injury, giving the address of the nearest minor injuries unit (MIU) in case further treatment is needed after the practitioner has applied first aid. When working with autistic learners a phone number of the MIU should be easily accessible and the practitioner should ring ahead to explain to the MIU that the casualty en route is autistic and may need support on arrival – for example, they may find it hard to wait and may need to be seen quickly due to anxiety.

The emergency procedure should also give details of how to evacuate a casualty from the woods in the event of a situation that requires an ambulance to be called. The procedure should give coordinates and directions to access points into the wood for the emergency services.

Finally, the emergency procedure should include what should be done in the event of a learner wandering away from the group and getting lost. This should ensure that the rest of the group are kept together and are safe while a search takes place.

The practitioner is responsible for ensuring that an emergency bag is present at all times. The emergency bag should contain a first-aid kit, a copy of the emergency procedure, a mobile phone and emergency contact details for all participants.

The environment

Natural settings can contain various hazards but it is important not to get carried away when considering them. All environments contain potential risks. The average house is chock full of danger if you choose to look for it – electric sockets to thrust fingers into, cleaning products to drink, stairs to fall down. Potential disaster is everywhere! Yet we usually feel safe and secure in houses. Why?

Because we are familiar with the environment, understand the potential hazards and know how to avoid them.

It's important to become familiar with the environment in which Forest School will take place and to learn what potential hazards it may hold. Different settings contain different types of flora and fauna, and the environment changes through the seasons. The practitioner needs to have an environmental risk assessment in place and to make a dynamic risk assessment of the site before sessions begin on the day.

Things to look for include the following areas:

- *Dead wood* – This may be on the ground, which presents little risk, other than tripping or sticks poking out at eye level. Standing dead wood (such as dead trees) may present a risk if climbed on, and hanging dead wood is the most potentially hazardous. Hanging dead wood may be larger dead branches that the wind has broken off, but which are caught up on other branches in the canopy. If these fall they can cause serious injury if they strike someone standing underneath. If dangerous hanging dead wood is seen then the practitioner should make sure that activities take place away from the area beneath the hazard and report it to the landowner or whoever is responsible for the maintenance.

- *Poisonous flora* – Practitioners should be aware of any potentially poisonous plants growing in the area where the session takes place. Common plants to be aware of in the UK include foxgloves, hemlock, deadly nightshade, lily of the valley, yew, holly berries, ivy and monkshood. Poisonous fungi include death cap, brown roll rim, false morel, panther cap and turban fungus. Remember that most of these plants or fungi appear seasonally and will not all be present throughout the year. The danger from these plants comes from their ingestion and the likelihood of this happening depends to a great extent on the individuals attending the session. If it is likely that a learner will attempt to eat flora or fungi then, as with the hanging dead wood described above, activities should take place away from the area in which the poisonous flora is growing. Some flora, such as nettles or giant hogweed, may cause skin irritations if touched, and again should be identified and avoided. Remember that for more able learners identifying that a particular plant should be avoided, and discussing why, is enough to ensure that they will self-manage risk.

- *Fauna* – In the UK, there is very little danger posed by large animals. In Chapter 4, we discussed dog phobias and how this can be managed. The main fauna which can cause harm are insects such as wasps, bees or mosquitoes, which can bite or sting. It is important to know if any participants have allergic reactions to bites or stings and if they need to bring an epipen with them. Stings and bites can be avoided by ensuring that legs and arms are covered throughout the year and insect repellent can be worn if required. These kinds of insects are only present in the UK during the warmer months. The greatest risk in the UK probably comes from ticks. Ticks hang on to the body and draw blood before falling off. The tick itself is not particularly harmful but they can carry Lyme disease, which is a serious illness. In woodland, ticks are spread by deer and areas of cover where deer are known to live are best avoided. As with other bugs, ensuring that long-sleeved tops and trousers are worn will also offer some protection.

- *Landscape considerations* – The practitioner should be aware of the lie of the land and if there is any still or running water, caves, steep drops or other potential hazards on site. Remember that these areas are as likely to be great resources for the group as sources of harm, and that a thorough risk assessment can ensure that learners can take part in activities such as pond dipping, playing Pooh sticks or even exploring a cave, as long as you can prove that you have taken all reasonable steps to minimise risk.

- *Setting boundaries* – Physical boundaries are set with the group, either by staff or, if possible, through negotiation with the learners. These boundaries ensure that no one wanders off and gets lost and that any areas with potential hazards are avoided by all participants. The best way to ensure that people remain within safe areas is to maintain a higher staffing level, either supporters, Forest School staff, or volunteers. The level of staffing needed will depend to some extent on the needs of the group. Some practitioners use a whistle to call the group together but this should only be done if you are certain that none of the learners has a sensory aversion to high-pitched noises. It may be more appropriate to consider how big a group can be safely managed and the different methods of communication that individual learners may require to remain within safe boundaries. In my experience, it is harder to encourage my autistic learners to explore outside a small area than to restrict them from wandering, but this must be judged on an individual basis.

The weather

Forest School takes place throughout the year and consideration must be given to the comfort of all participants. If someone is cold, wet or too hot there will be little chance of them benefiting from Forest School!

People attending will need to be dressed appropriately. They will need stout, waterproof footwear throughout the year and access to waterproofs for wet weather. The practitioner will need to decide if these will be supplied by Forest School or if participants will be asked to bring their own with them.

In hot weather, participants will need to wear light clothing but will need to have long sleeves and trousers to protect from biting insects and scratches or stings from plants. Make sure that there is enough clean drinking water available and participants have sun block, but be aware of any restrictions on applying suncream which may be required by the participant's school or service.

Once inside the woods it is usually cooler and there is often natural shade beneath trees, but extra shade can be quickly supplied by tying a tarpaulin up between trees. Some practitioners may choose to build semi-permanent shelters that protect from the sun, wind and rain. This is discussed further in Chapter 10.

In cold weather, it is important that learners are properly dressed. This means layers of warm clothing and waterproofs are required. Activities should be planned that minimise sitting still, unless this is around a warming fire – remember the old saying: 'A fire warms you three times: once when you collect the wood, again when you saw the wood, and finally when you warm yourself by it.' Getting wet or being exposed to wind makes people colder so it is important that clothes are waterproof and windproof and that there is a suitable level of shelter available.

Whenever the weather is particularly hot or cold you should observe learners closely for signs of discomfort. Forest School is not an endurance test. If someone appears to be adversely affected by the weather, despite all precautions being taken to ensure that they are safe, then it's best to call a close to their session. If the level of supervision allows, then they may leave the group individually, otherwise it may be necessary to bring the whole session to a halt. This should rarely be the case if the practitioner has planned ahead properly and ensured that adequate measures have been put in place but it's always possible that a surprise may crop up, such as someone soaking themselves to the skin by falling in a puddle on a cold day.

There may be occasions when the weather causes the session to be cancelled. The practitioner should have an inclement weather procedure in place which gives details of measures to take in the event of a cancellation. The most disruptive weather conditions are high winds. It is not safe to be beneath trees if the winds are forecast to be too strong. Weather websites will inform in advance of these conditions and the session should be cancelled. I would not recommend trying to judge on the day as there may be lulls in the storm, or it may arrive later than forecast, requiring you to evacuate the woods during a session and causing unnecessary stress to your group. Bear in mind that autistic people need as much notice as possible if their routine is changed, so you need to let participants know as soon as the decision is made to ensure that they have time to process the situation.

The activities

The level of risk inherent in an activity depends partly on the abilities of the participants, including the competence of the practitioner and supporters. This is considered on an individual basis and progresses over time. New practitioners should not worry if they aren't experienced in all aspects of outdoor pursuits. Sessions can be planned to play to your strengths and expand as you learn new skills; sometimes these may be taught to you by learners or supporters, who will bring their own skills and abilities with them.

The most potentially harmful activities at Forest School generally involve tool use and fire. Safety procedures around fire are discussed fully in Chapter 10, when we consider different activities.

Likely injury from tools takes two forms: impact injuries or cuts. Both of these are much less likely to occur if tools are used in a safe way. The practitioner needs to learn how to use tools safely, model safety in their own tool use and teach safe handling to the group. Sometimes learners may struggle to use tools safely on their own, either due to being very young or due to impairment, but there are still methods in which they can be supported to use tools.

Tool use can be built up to slowly. As observations show the gross and fine motor skills and sensory perception of the learner it becomes clearer how ready they may be to begin to use tools and what level of support they may need to do so.

The practitioner must know what tools are present and their whereabouts throughout the session. There are different ways to achieve this depending on the size of the group and the level of independence of the learners. Some practitioners sign tools in and out of the tool bag, the person signing the tool out taking responsibility for ensuring that it is returned. This may not be necessary with smaller groups if tools can be kept track of while observing the learners.

The main tools used at my Forest School are bowsaws, pruning saws, knives, billhooks and hammers. There is plenty of potential for bloodshed and bruising there, unless we ensure that safe procedures are followed.

Before any tool is taken to a session, a risk assessment must be in place which is specific to that tool and sometimes it may be be necessary to have a personal risk assessment in place for the individual who will be using the tool.

Once I have observed learners taking part in low-risk activities and I feel that I'm beginning to establish trust and some knowledge of their abilities, I introduce tools to the group. The first introduction to tools is a safety talk. Whenever I give the talk I try to ensure that I am consistent in the order in which I present the information and I may reinforce the talk with visual boards or Social Stories™ if this is more effective for individual learners. Some learners may gain better safety understanding if supporters lead them through safe tool use every time the tool is used.

First, a safety talk needs to cover wearing safety gloves or any other personal protective equipment (PPE) required to handle the tool. When safety gloves are worn, it is best to only wear them on the hand which is holding whatever is being worked on. The hand holding the tool will have a better grip if it is bare. Sometimes learners may not be able to wear gloves due to tactile hypersensitivity. In this case, you could consider a supporter wearing gloves holding the object being worked on, while the learner uses the tool. It's important that the learner's free hand is kept away from the business end of the tool; ask them to hold the free hand by their side or on the supporter's shoulder.

The safety talk should show how to take tools from the bag and how to take off and replace any safety guards or safely fold and how to lock folding tools, such as penknives or pruning saws. A lot of cuts occur from mishandling safety guards or clumsily trying to fold a blade back into the tool handle, so it is important that learners are shown the correct techniques for handling and are taught to ensure that safety guards are in place, or tools folded, when carrying them across site or whenever they are not in use.

Learners should be shown how to safely pass the tool from one person to another, ensuring that nobody takes hold of the cutting part of any tool.

Correct use of the tool should then be demonstrated. This should not only cover the technique for tool use but also the need for other people to keep a safe distance from any person using a tool. This is usually defined as 'two arm lengths and one tool length' away from the person.

Learners should be taught to return tools to the tool bag when they have finished using them.

Remember that following routines is often a strength that comes with autism. Try to present the safety routine as a consistent system. Autistic learners will often find it easier to follow safety procedures than neurotypical learners, the exception to this being people with poor impulse control. If someone has poor impulse control then the practitioner should write an individual risk assessment for them that puts extra measures in place (such as close one-to-one support and keeping tools in a lockable bag).

Forest School's origins in working with early years children has led to the development of various techniques and accommodations that help people who may have less well-developed fine or gross motor skills to take part in tool use. We can still offer opportunities for joining in to people who may struggle to be completely independent in tool use by utilising these techniques. For example:

- *Two-person sawing* – This requires a saw such as a bowsaw or hacksaw which has a frame above the blade. The learner holds the handle and a supporter holds the frame at the opposite end of the saw. Before sawing the supporter may need to make a 'plunge cut' into the wood to be sawed. This is just a matter of making a small cut of a few strokes which the blade can be put back into to ensure that the learner saws the right spot and the blade does not bounce around. The supporter, holding the frame at one end of the saw while the learner holds the handle at the other end helps to guide the learner's saw strokes, working in a gentle rhythm together. If an autistic learner has been observed to use rocking motions to stim then a gentle rocking of the upper body can accompany the saw strokes but be careful not to encourage more vigorous rocking. Keep in mind that systems can be physical too, and encourage fluid and consistent movement.

- *Using a strike to split wood* – Learners can help to split wood, either for the fire or as part of green woodwork projects (such as the Gypsy Furniture described in Chapter 10). The practitioner should choose where the wood will be split and tap the billhook into the end just enough for it to bite into the wood in the correct place. The learner can then use a short and stout piece of wood to tap on the top edge of the billhook while the practitioner holds the handle. This should only be attempted if the learner will be reasonably accurate with their tapping.

For some learners, these types of techniques will be a stepping stone to more independent tool use but if this is not possible then these methods can remain in place as accommodations that ensure inclusive practice. One of my great delights is the look of achievement on learners' faces when we have worked together to saw through wood and the saw has just cut right through!

Any other activities that have the potential to cause harm will need to be risk assessed and all reasonable measures put in place to reduce the risk of harm. For example, hammocks need to be anchored to points that are strong enough to bear the weight, and knots should be secure. Hammocks should not be more than 50cm above the ground and the area beneath them must be free from obstructions. Learners need to sit or lie in the hammocks, and not stand or jump in them, so they may require supervision.

Chapter 10 discusses some typical Forest School activities and covers some of the safety issues for the practitioner to be aware of.

The individual

The learners in any group may have individual needs that need to be taken into account when planning sessions. In Chapter 4, we mentioned some of the individual health issues that need to be considered when preparing sessions. Some of these, such as allergies or food intolerances, may be encountered in any learner, but some conditions are more specific to autistic learners and warrant closer consideration.

Sensory differences

In the last chapter, we covered the differences in sensory perception that are experienced by many autistic people. I would suggest that the practitioner thinks of adverse reactions to sensory stimuli in the same way as other safety concerns. Although other people may not be experiencing the discomfort felt by the person who has a sensory aversion, from the perspective of that person, it is entirely real. No practitioner would dream of making a learner walk through a nettle patch wearing a pair of shorts, because they know from their own experience of nettle stings how horrible this would feel. Yet neurotypical people do, sometimes, encourage autistic people they are supporting to continue in situations in which the autistic person is clearly uncomfortable and unhappy. Usually this is inadvertent and happens due to a lack of understanding of exactly what is causing the problem, as the neurotypical person is not experiencing it themselves and lacks awareness of other sensory perceptions. In the same way as you plan to minimise risks and put measures in place to lessen their impact, you will need to plan accommodations to lessen any exposure to unpleasant stimuli. Remember that sensory profiles are individual and different people will require different accommodations. Be flexible in your approach. For example, if someone cannot wear a waterproof coat due to tactile sensitivity then could they use an umbrella? Or is it a particular type of coat that is uncomfortable? Perhaps a different kind of waterproof fabric would be better – sometimes it is simply a label inside the coat that is causing irritation and this can be removed. Be ready to think outside the box to find solutions if you need to.

Temperature and pain

Some autistic people experience differences in how they perceive temperature. Some people do not feel the cold to the extent that others do and this can sometimes be the reason that a learner is reluctant to wear a coat rather than issues with tactile hypersensitivity. Some learners may also be hyposensitive to pain and have very high pain thresholds. In either case, it is important to closely monitor the learner and ensure that they are not showing signs of discomfort, as they may become too cold before they realise or could have picked up an injury and not indicated to anyone that they require first aid.

Pica

This describes the eating of items that are not food and hold no nutritious value. When considering whether a learner is presenting behaviours which meet the criteria for pica you should try to ascertain whether they are actually ingesting whatever items they are putting to their mouths or if they are tasting them or feeling their texture and firmness using their mouths and then spitting them out. If learners are ingesting items, this increases the level of risk from toxic flora to a great extent. As suggested when we considered the environmental risks, it's vital to be aware of what is growing in the area, and the potential toxicity of the plants present. If a learner mouths objects there will need to be enough supporters present to ensure that they are constantly monitored and activities should be offered in areas where there are no potentially dangerous plants or objects present. Don't get things out of perspective though. People who mouth or ingest objects generally do so in all environments, with all types of objects. The objects found in natural environments aren't necessarily more harmful than the type of indigestible things found in manmade environments.

Motor skills

Some autistic people display differences in their physical coordination and have difficulty carrying out fine or gross motor tasks. The practitioner needs to be aware of how this can affect activities, such as tool use, and give the learner the time and space to carry out these kinds of tasks without feeling pressured, ensuring that proper safety procedures are adhered to and protective equipment, such as safety gloves, are always used.

Epilepsy

There is a higher prevalence of epilepsy in autistic people than in the general population and it's important to be aware of whether any of the group has epilepsy before sessions begin. People with epilepsy are prone to having seizures. Most people are aware of tonic clonic seizures, which affect the whole brain and cause the person to lose consciousness and their body to convulse, but may be less aware of other types of seizure.

Generalised seizures affect the whole brain and focal seizures affect one part of the brain. People remain conscious during focal seizures; if a smaller part of the brain is affected then they will remember the seizure but if a larger part of the brain is affected they may become confused and uncommunicative. Behaviours observed can include rubbing clothes with the fingers, talking to people who aren't there, disorientation and sometimes panic. Generalised seizures may present as:

- absences, when the person suddenly becomes uncommunicative due to losing consciousness for a short period but with very few physical symptoms

- the body stiffening (tonic), or going floppy (atonic), which may cause a person to fall to the ground.

Myoclonic seizures are sudden involuntary jerks of the body. Tonic clonic seizures are when the body initially goes stiff then into convulsions.

Before beginning sessions with epileptic learners, the practitioner should be clear on how to respond to a seizure. Seizures are triggered by different things in different people but common triggers include tiredness, overheating and stress. The practitioner should be aware of any triggers and try to avoid them. The practitioner will need to be aware of what kind of seizures the person has and how frequently they happen and then risk assess accordingly. The practitioner should find out from supporters what protocol is in place in event of seizure, and how they are required to respond. In the UK, epilepsy nurses work with the person and their supporters to put an individual written protocol in place which sets out how to respond to that person's seizures. This will often include a time frame after which the emergency services must be called if a person remains in seizure. The practitioner must have a robust emergency procedure in place, which includes access points to the site for the ambulance service, to ensure that any casualty can be evacuated in a worst-case scenario.

Some behaviour seen in seizures, such as absences or focal seizures, can outwardly appear to be very similar to behaviours presented due to autism, such as seeming not to be paying attention to others or rubbing fingers over clothes. It's important that the practitioner records and evidences these observations and shares them with other supporters, so that the possibility that these particular behaviours are caused by epilepsy can be considered by professionals, if they occur in a pattern which suggests that this may be the case.

Safety first

The practitioner should have safety in mind at all times but must learn to reinforce safety in a positive way. We *do not* want a situation where the practitioner is constantly barking out, 'NO!' or, 'DON'T DO THAT!' or, 'YOU'LL HAVE SOMEONE'S EYE OUT WITH THAT!' every 30 seconds. When you need to reinforce safe practice use positive language, for example if someone is using a saw incorrectly say, 'Use it like this' rather than 'Don't use it like that.' Lead by example and be consistent.

When reading through a chapter detailing health and safety concerns it's hard not to take a sharp intake of breath and worry that the whole thing is a terrible, dangerous, business after all! This really isn't the case in practice! Prior consideration and planning minimise the risk of things going wrong and ensure that the practitioner is ready to respond appropriately to any problems that may occur. Don't underestimate the ability of autistic learners to self-manage risk. People attending my sessions are generally as likely to be over-cautious as reckless, and evidencing an individual's ability to self-manage risk can help to reassure their supporters and increase their confidence in opening up new opportunities for the learner. If people have safe procedures reinforced consistently from the start, then everyone (including the practitioner) will be able to enjoy the sessions.

KEY POINTS

▶ Risk is inherent in most activities. Avoiding any activity that may contain an element of risk has a detrimental effect because it removes the opportunity to take part in many beneficial activities. This is true of everyone but particularly in the case of people who have perceived disabilities and this is explicit in best-practice approaches.

▶ In order to view risk positively we must show that we have taken all reasonable steps to minimise risks beforehand. Creating risk assessments before activities take place is an important tool in minimising risk. Risk assessments are ongoing and should change as circumstances change. They should be viewed as a way to give people the opportunity to do things and not as a way to deny people those opportunities.

▶ The practitioner should be trained in first aid and have a robust emergency procedure in place that details how to respond to injuries or a learner going missing, including emergency evacuation by ambulance. An emergency bag should be present containing a first-aid kit, a copy of the emergency procedure, a mobile phone and emergency contact details for all participants.

▶ The practitioner needs to familiar with any possible hazards in the environment and to have risk assessed these and put procedures in place to minimise risk.

▶ The weather should be considered and all participants need to be comfortable whatever the conditions. Adequate shelter and shade are needed and sessions must be planned to take conditions into account.

▶ Activities are tailored to the needs of learners, and activities that contain a greater element of risk should not be introduced immediately but gradually, as the practitioner becomes aware of the learner's needs and abilities.

- ▶ Accommodations can be made, for instance techniques of tool use such as two-person sawing, to ensure that less able people can still take part in activities safely.

- ▶ The practitioner needs to be aware of any factors that are specific to individuals and may present risk. There are some conditions, such as sensory issues, pica and epilepsy, which are more prevalent among autistic people, and these must be planned for in advance.

- ▶ Prior planning and training reduce risk and prepare the practitioner for how to respond if things do go wrong.

CHAPTER 9

Setting up a
Forest School

If you are not already involved with Forest School and have read this far then I hope you now want to find out how you can get out into the woods and take part in Forest School. The two main options are to join an existing group or to set up your own.

Joining an existing group

This is a good option for someone who wants to take part in Forest School and lives in an area where there are existing groups which suit their needs. When seeking a group, it's important to find a practitioner who is properly trained and insured and who is prepared to work together with the learner and their supporters to meet their needs and make any accommodations that may be required.

In my opinion, partnership working is vital in ensuring that autistic learners benefit from Forest School. The practitioner should be open to partnership working from the outset. Ideally, they should be asking the type of questions suggested in Chapter 4 of this book, or open to discussing the learner's needs well in advance of sessions beginning. Supporters should be prepared to help the practitioner get to know and understand the learner. You should expect the practitioner to directly involve the learner in preparation as much as they can, if it is possible to do so.

There is a great deal of variance in the levels of autism awareness displayed by Forest School practitioners. People come to Forest School from different disciplines and don't necessarily have much previous experience of autism, but in my experience most practitioners are very committed to ensuring positive outcomes for all their learners and are keen to learn how to accommodate autistic participants. Obviously, prior experience of running autism-inclusive sessions is desirable but may not be essential if supporters are going to attend sessions with the learner and provide the necessary support to both learner and practitioner to ensure that sessions go well.

Starting your own group

Setting up a Forest School group is not difficult and support is available to help newcomers to get started. This is a good option if you are already providing a service to autistic people through school, day service or social group.

The first step is to find a qualified Forest School practitioner to lead your sessions. This may involve finding someone who is already qualified and buying them in to provide sessions. Your service can provide additional training to the practitioner if they have little prior experience of autism. If a service chooses to buy in a qualified practitioner, it is important that they are prepared to work in partnership with the practitioner. I can't emphasise enough that partnership working is an important factor in how much benefit an autistic learner takes from Forest School. This is, perhaps, less important if the learner has good skills in self-advocacy, but even if this isn't the case it should not be overlooked.

The other option is to choose a member of staff or existing supporter and fund their Forest School training. This option guarantees that your practitioner will be autism aware and, just as importantly, have an existing relationship with the learners.

Forest School training

In order to lead Forest School sessions, you require a Level Three Forest School Practitioner qualification. In addition, you are also required to have a two-day outdoor first-aid qualification.

In the UK, there is quite a wide choice of different training providers with some variance of course content. A Level Three course will cover the ethos and some of the theory behind the Forest School pedagogy, encourage awareness of the environment and introduce practical skills. By the end of the course the practitioner should have everything in place to begin to deliver sessions.

People come to Forest School from different disciplines. Some have a background in education, some work with people in different support capacities and some come from a background in nature management and conservation. You do not need to be an expert in all of these areas but you do need to have a willingness to learn about the areas where you lack experience.

The Level Three course usually takes between six months and a year to complete, comprising about a week based in the classroom and woods with instructors, with other learning taking place in your work setting and through home study. If you choose to train a member of your own team then they must be willing to make a commitment to completing the course. Good course providers offer support and advice after the course is completed.

Finding a site

Forest School needs to take place in an outdoor setting, preferably among woodland. In some settings, there may be green space in the grounds of the school or service that would be suitable for use. This can be a good option if Forest School is taking place within a timetable of school lessons or day service activities, as it is easy to access. However, unless there is a wood on site, this can also be limiting in relation to the natural resources available to use in sessions and you may need to consider bringing resources to the session from elsewhere.

Another option is to arrange permission to use public woodland. UK organisations such as the Forestry Commission or Woodland Trust are supportive of community use of the woodland they manage and will often give practitioners support and guidance on minimising environmental impact and using the wood's natural resources responsibly. In urban areas, small woods can be found in public parks or on council-owned land. The drawback of using public woodland is that you share the space with the rest of the community! This increases the chance of your site being interfered with between sessions and of disturbances from dog walkers. Some public woodland can be very busy at certain times of the day and this needs to be considered if any of your learners are afraid of dogs.

Private woodland is a good option. Many landowners are very approachable if you present yourself in a professional manner and demonstrate an awareness of safety and a responsible attitude. Private woodland may still have public rights of way crossing it and you should discuss this with the landowner to discover if any areas of the land are used by dog walkers, and also find out if any other people use the site for other activities and if you need to make arrangements to fit in around this.

When choosing a site, you should consider the following aspects:

- *Accessibility* – How will the group reach the site. If you are travelling by motor vehicle is there somewhere safe to park? Is the site accessible by emergency services? Is the site accessible for any learners with mobility issues?

- *Hazards* – What potential hazards are present? Are there ponds, caves, cliffs or any similar hazards? Can risk be minimised? Remember that potential hazards can become potential resources once risk assessments are put in place.

- *Environmental aspects* – Will your sessions have a negative environmental impact? Does the site contain rare flora or fauna that should not be disturbed? Can you ensure that this will not happen? If not then you should consider a different site.

- *Landowners' permissions* – What activities will the landowner allow? You should be specific about this from the outset. Don't assume that permission to use a site allows you to do whatever you want there. Are fires permitted? Can you collect dead wood? Can you cut any green wood? Are there any areas that are out of bounds? Be very clear on all boundaries and permissions from the very beginning to avoid any misunderstandings. Show an awareness of safety and environmental sustainability. Practitioners should work with landowners to draw up an environmental impact assessment and management plan before sessions begin.

The Forest School Association

I would strongly recommend that practitioners join the Forest School Association (FSA).

The origin of the FSA and the Principles and Criteria for Good Practice are discussed in Chapter 1. FSA membership allows the practitioner to network and share practice and gives access to further training and workshops to help develop skills and awareness of different aspects of Forest School.

The FSA is currently developing a scheme to endorse Forest School providers and trainers in the UK and is a good port of call for any school or service seeking to find a practitioner to run sessions.

The FSA website can be found at: www.forestschoolassociation.org.

KEY POINTS

▶ The two main options if you are interested in accessing Forest School are joining an existing group or starting your own.

▶ If you choose to join an existing group then it is important to find a practitioner who will work in partnership with the learner and their supporters.

- ▶ If you already have a group who would like to begin Forest School then you have a choice of finding a qualified practitioner, who may need further autism-awareness training, or providing Forest School training to a member of your staff team.

- ▶ To lead Forest School sessions, you need a Level Three Forest School Pracitioner qualification and an outdoor first-aid qualification.

- ▶ Forest School training will cover the ethos of Forest School, practical skills, environmental awareness and health and safety. Once qualified, the practitioner will have everything in place to begin running sessions.

- ▶ Forest School sites can be found in different settings. Some groups may have access to the grounds of their school or service, and some may negotiate to use public or private woodland. Areas of woodland can be found in urban locations in parks or council-owned land.

- ▶ When choosing a site, consider if it meets the needs of your group, is accessible and safe and if natural resources are present that you are allowed to use.

- ▶ Always consider and plan for environmental sustainability.

- ▶ It is recommended that practitioners join the Forest School Association.

CHAPTER 10

Forest School Activities

So, we've completed our preparations. We're qualified. We're insured. We've arranged access to our site and, it is hoped, have some learners who want to attend. Our policies, procedures and risk assessments are in place. We've got any background information we need about our learners and have thought through how best to begin to tailor our sessions to them. What's next?

Well, now it's time for the fun bit.

In our first session, we need to establish boundaries, introduce safety routines and encourage the group to explore the site. In this initial session, it is important to remember that you are establishing the structure which sessions will follow from here on in. It is to be hoped that you have prepared learners and any staff for what to expect and you have ensured that you are familiar with their needs and preferences. You should ensure consistency in the routine parts of session structure from the start.

This is an example of the structure of one of my sessions:

- Check over the site before the session ensuring there are no hazards of which I was previously unaware.

- Meet the group in the car park. Make sure everyone is changed into appropriate clothing and has everything they may need during the session (lunch, medicines, any items that a person may need to carry with them).

- Distribute kit to be carried. Walk across the fields and down into the woods to our Forest School site.

- When the group have gathered, stop and close our eyes for a moment of quiet listening (easier said than done sometimes!).

- Brief the group about the day's choices of activity and reinforce safety procedures.

- Begin the activity and support, observe and encourage as appropriate, take evidence photographs, praise achievements.

- Put on the kettle and eat lunch.

- Eat and drink together, reflect with the group on the session.

- Extinguish all fires.

- Clear up site. Ensure all tools and kit are accounted for.

- Carry kit back to the car park.

- Thank everyone for coming and say, 'Goodbye and see you next week.'

This structure is consistent from session to session. Different sessions tend to develop additional details in the structure based on the preferences of the learners.

The activities I will describe in this chapter are some of the basics common to Forest School sessions. They should be viewed as a starting point for practitioners who are just starting out in Forest School. They are suitable for most groups but you should remember to be person centred in your planning and to design your session around learning about and implementing the needs of your learners rather than imposing a template on them. The only limits to the activities you offer to your learners should be their abilities and your creativity.

Remember to keep sight of the basics:

- Communicate in a way that your learners can understand and allow them processing time.

- Give learners time and space if they need it. Sometimes less is more. Try to avoid pressurising anyone – it will only increase their stress.

- Do people understand what is expected of them and what is going to happen next? Establish predictability and structure.

- Be aware of sensory issues.

- Don't make assumptions.

- Forest School should be learner led. Always be ready to forget your lesson plan and follow your learner. You will often make your most valuable observations when they are creating their own activity.

- Recognise all achievements that members of your group make. Plan for opportunities to say 'Well done!' and recognise progression.

- This is the most important one. Have fun. Bring joy and a sense of humour. Is your group happy? All your sessions may not work out as planned but if people are happy, and you have kept them safe, then the session is a success and the learners will have benefited. You can reflect on how to improve for next time.

ACTIVITY 1: SENSORY COLLECTING

Suitable for: All ages and abilities

Resources: Something to collect items on – card with a strip of double-sided sticky tape along the middle is good but you can collect in boxes, bags or on trays

Benefits: Communication, choosing, sensory stimuli and observation, fine motor skills, exercise

This activity is a great way to encourage your group to explore their surroundings and find their bearings on your site.

Decide before the session what your learners will use to collect the items. Card with a strip of double-sided tape is great as people can create a display of their items as they go along but you can use little boxes, bags or trays if you like.

How much guidance is required for the activity will depend on the abilities of the group and how much staff support there is.

If the group is able then you can give them a theme to their collecting. This could be based on senses – for example, a colour, something rough, something smooth.

Ensure that your communication meets the needs of your group. Can everyone understand the information in the way that you are presenting it? Do you need to use any other communication systems? Do people have any staff or carers with them who can help them to understand, or should you observe closely so that you can support if required?

People may find this easier to understand if you have a clearly stated number of items for people to collect.

Once you have communicated the theme, the group can explore and look for items.

Make sure you have set the boundaries before the activity begins – for example, not wandering out of sight, not picking or damaging living plants.

For less able groups, support workers can support people to explore the site and understand the task. Make sure that support workers are offering a choice to the learners about what they collect and are engaging them. They may have to offer a binary choice holding two items up so that the learner can indicate their choice.

Encourage learners of all abilities to explore the sensory aspects of the things they collect – touch, visual, smell, any noise the item can make.

If there are not enough support workers present to support a less able group to explore then you can take the lead and guide the group on a sensory walk around your site. Stop and give the group items to explore and encourage them to choose which ones they want to keep.

Once all the learners have collected all the items gather the group together in a circle.

Encourage the group to take turns displaying their items. If they have used card and double-sided tape their items are already displayed; if not, lay out a tarpaulin or surface which the items can be arranged on to be displayed.

Encourage learners to explore the sensory aspects of one anothers items.

Encourage and facilitate communication between the members of the group.

Praise the learners for good participation.

ACTIVITY 2: LEAF RUBBING

Suitable for: All ages and abilities

Resources: Crayons, pencils or charcoal, paper, clipboards

Benefits: Communication, fine motor skills, sensory stimuli and proprioceptive observation, learning about different trees, making choices, categorising

I love this activity. It can be enjoyed on a simple, basic level but can be expanded upon to suit any age or ability.

Make sure you have planned to do this at a time of the year when there will be leaves! Begin by giving each learner a clipboard and paper and let them choose a colour of crayon.

Walk with the group through the wood and stop to make leaf rubbings. Simply place the leaf on your clipboard, put the paper over the top and then colour over the top with your crayon to bring out the outline of the leaf.

This will produce lovely outlines of the different leaves you have chosen. Learners with impaired fine motor skills or physical disabilities may need some hands-on support to help them to achieve this but can still enjoy this activity.

This is a great way to begin to identify different trees. If you are quite new to identifying trees yourself then this is a good way to learn along with your group. When identifying different types of tree you can introduce the group to the idea of diversity. A forest is made up of different types of tree in the same way as our communities are made up of different types of people. All the different trees belong in the forest and it's the same with our communities.

Some autistic learners may show strength in categorising things and they may enjoy creating a record of their leaf rubbings that notes the species of tree and other details. These records can be taken back to the woods, in later sessions, and used to identify trees and any changes which have taken place during the time since the rubbings were first made.

Some learners may prefer to make freehand pencil sketches of the leaves you have found.

Some learners may have a sensory need for 'messy play' and may like to dip leaves in paint then press them on the paper.

You could combine this with a charcoal-making activity and use the charcoal you have made to make leaf rubbings.

ACTIVITY 3: ESTABLISHING A BASE?

Suitable for: All ages and abilities

Resources: Not required

Benefits: Communication, working as a team, planning ahead, exercise

The first thing to ask yourself before planning this activity is, 'Do I want to have a base?' Some Forest School practitioners choose not to have a base area and prefer to establish a different base camp in each session depending on which area of their site they're using, leaving no trace of themselves when they leave the woods.

I would recommend having a base camp that stays in the same place. I feel that walking to the same spot at the start of a session helps to establish a predictable structure. If learners have chosen a quiet spot which they can retreat to if they feel stressed it's better if they can find their bearings to get there easily, taking into account that they may be experiencing difficulties with sensory processing at these times. It is also worth taking into account that you may need to be based near enough to access points if you have learners with a history of epilepsy that has required calling out the ambulance service.

If possible, try to involve your group in choosing the best site for your base camp. Consider the size of your group and choose an area large enough for everyone to sit in a square or circle around a central fire pit. Ensure that there is enough space for people to walk around the outside and not through the fire pit area if they have to change position.

When choosing the site, try to imagine what it will be like in different weather conditions and seasons. Will it become waterlogged after heavy rain? Is there enough shade on really hot days? Avoid areas where animals can be seen to have their homes or wild flowers such as bluebells are established. Try to make sure that the whole group is involved in this process.

Is the site suitable for all members of your group? Does anyone have mobility issues? Do you need to ensure wheelchair access?

Remember to make sure that looking for a site is fun! You're not building the pyramids! If you do choose a site that ends up under water after the first heavy shower, it's okay. Just move to a new spot. It's all an adventure. Don't become so paranoid about any slight change impacting on your autistic learner that you become the person who is rigid and inflexible. If changes are effectively communicated and the rest of the structure is consistent you'll probably do fine!

Set out the area where you will have your fire pit. Put a boundary around the fire area using rocks or green wood and clear a layer of soil inside the fire pit. Make sure there is ample clearance above the fire – you don't want to be setting overhanging branches on fire!

Mark where the seating area will be. This needs to be 1.5 metres away from the fire pit. You may put logs or stumps for people to sit on if these are available to you or you may mark the seating area with a line of sticks if your group are sitting on cushions or a tarpaulin that you will take away after each session. Clear all the sticks, twigs or brash inside your fire square to make sure your fire won't spread and ensure there are no trip hazards. If the ground is peat or pine needles, be aware that it can ignite and smoulder and consider having your fire in a firebowl or on a metal tray.

A tip worth considering when establishing a base is the 'structured classroom' approach used in some schools. Classrooms are partitioned and different areas are used for different activities. There may be a reading area, an art area and a maths area. This physically compartmentalised approach can help some autistic learners to better understand which activity they are expected to be taking part in and help them to focus on the task. You could have clearly marked areas of your base camp for circle time, tool use, quiet areas and so on.

Get your entire group involved. Remember to differentiate tasks and support as required.

Shelter can be provided by tarpaulins, hung from the trees on the day, or you may choose to build sustainable structures, such as bender tents, if the landowner permits.

That is your basic base camp set up. Never lose sight of trying to tread lightly. A fire pit can be covered back over and any seating returned to where you found it. Any natural structures can be dismantled and the site can be quickly returned to nature. Some established Forest School providers have more permanent structures on their sites; some do not like to leave anything that outlasts one session. Take into consideration the needs of your group and try to involve them in the choice – don't forget it's their session.

ACTIVITY 4: KELLY KETTLES

Suitable for: All ages and abilities

Resources: Kelly kettle, fire steel, tinder, hot drinks, cups, spoons, water, milk

Benefits: Communication, fine motor skills, sensory stimuli, learning about fire safety, making choices, independence

Ask any group of learners who attend Forest School what they like best and I can guarantee that at least one of them will reply 'hot chocolate'! There's no nicer way to finish a session on a cold day than by making and having a hot drink. You can bring hot water to site with you in flasks, boil a kettle on the fire or use a kelly kettle.

Kelly kettles are also known as storm kettles or ghillie kettles and are a quick and easy way to boil water when you are outdoors. The kettle consists of two sections, a base pan with an air hole in the side and the kettle itself. The kettle is hollow inside with a hole at the top and the outer walls of the kettle are a sleeve which contains the water. A fire is lit in the base pan and the kettle then fits on top. The fire heats up the inner walls of the kettle, which have the water behind them, and the large surface area ensures that the water boils quickly.

Kelly kettles are a great way to introduce the use of fire to sessions. You can assess the behaviour of people around fire and ensure that safety procedures are understood and followed.

Once the kettle is lit you will very quickly find yourself with fire, boiling water, hot metal and your learners all in close proximity. It is important that all safety considerations have been understood and met before any fire is lit.

The group must be given a full safety talk at the start of this activity. Show the group the kettle and explain how it is used and the safety boundaries:

- Explain the fire triangle – a fire needs air, heat and fuel.

- The metal will get hot enough to burn and must not be touched.

- Hands must not be placed above the hole on the top of the kettle when it is on top of the base pan. Even if the fire seems to have died down, a sudden breeze may cause flames to shoot out of the top hole.

- Fuel the fire through the top hole with small sticks by resting the stick on the lip of the top hole then carefully tilting it and dropping it in, ensuring that your hand does not go over the top hole.

- Do not allow the spout to face anyone – hot water may spit out if it boils quickly (make sure the spout is on the opposite side to the air hole in the base pan in case you have to gently blow inside to encourage the fire).

- Don't allow people to crowd around the fire at any time. Introduce the rules for using fire. The group should be 1.5 metres away from the fire at all times and should only come closer if invited to do so.

- The kettle should be placed on level ground and any brash cleared around to ensure that the fire cannot spread out of the pan. Have water at hand just in case.

- When the kettle is being placed on or removed from the fire it should be lifted by holding the handle at right angles to the body of the kettle and pushing the sides of the handle in towards one another. The hand should never be holding the handle above the top hole of the kettle while it is on the fire pan.

- Kelly kettles have a cork or rubber bung attached to a chain. This is placed in the spout when the kettle is not in use to make sure nothing gets into the water chamber. It must not be left in when the kettle goes on the fire pan.

- As soon as the kettle comes off the fire I douse the fire pan with water to put the fire out. Make sure it is safe and that no members of the group are going to go near it until it has cooled.

- After being taken off the fire pan the kettle is poured by holding the handle and lifting the chain. Make sure that cups are placed on a level surface and are not being held in people's hands. If you've got this far you don't want to scald people with spilt water!

- Remember that the kettle will be hot until it has had time to cool, so make sure it cannot be touched by learners.

Remember that some learners may find it easier to understand the safety procedure if you break it down and produce a visual communication sheet for them or put it in the form of a Social Story™. People with more severe learning impairments may not understand the whole safety procedure but can still take part as long as their support understands how to keep them safe during the activity.

Once you are satisfied that your group understands the safety issues you can begin to involve them in the process of using the kettle. Remember that if you break down activities then all learners will be able to contribute something to the overall process. If learners cannot be involved in the lighting or fuelling of the fire they can still be involved in collecting kindling, snapping it to size, filling the kettle with water and preparing drinks.

The activity should begin with the group collecting small dead sticks to fuel the fire with. The sticks need to be dry and vary in size from the thickness of a mouse's tail to about the thickness of a pencil. The group can break the sticks down to about 5–10cm long and grade them in size.

Build a 'waffle' in the base pan by crossing sticks over each other two at a time like a three-dimensional noughts and crosses board.

This is to allow air to be drawn in under the fire through the hole in the base pan, which will help your fire get going.

Make sure that all your fuel is close to hand but not somewhere where there is any risk of it being accidentally lit by any burning pieces that may escape from the base pan.

Fluff up your tinder (cotton wool is the easiest tinder to source) and use the fire steel to flick sparks onto it. If the air is damp, and it is reluctant to take, you can take a knife and gently scrape off tiny shavings of the fire steel onto the tinder. These will help to catch the sparks. If the weather is wet and people are struggling, you can always pop a little piece of fire lighter in. Remember that challenges need to be achievable!

Once the tinder catches the spark, carefully place a handful of the thinnest pieces of your wood on the fire. I like to mix some fast-burn material, such as dried dead nettle stalks, among this. As this catches, add slightly thicker pieces.

Once the fire is established in the pan, place the kettle on top following the safety procedure and fuel through the top hole as necessary, again ensuring that safe practice is observed. Remember to make sure that the spout and base pan air hole are on different sides and that the air hole is facing the breeze. Remember that on windy days the fire may really get going if it is blowing directly into the air hole and consider if you want to angle it away from the direct wind.

Before learners try this activity themselves I would recommend that they demonstrate that they can handle the kettle safely and fuel it correctly in a run through without any fire being lit. You shouldn't proceed until you are satisfied that they understand how to use the kettle safely.

When learners begin to carry out this task they will need one-to-one supervision and any staff helping them must be familiar with all of the safety issues for using a kettle. If appropriate, then the level of support can be withdrawn as the learner demonstrates safe practice and competence and they move towards independent use.

When being supported to use a kettle, the learner will need to use communication skills and turn taking and show patience.

Some autistic people have a tendency to find it difficult to judge how much to fuel the kettle and tend to be 'all or nothing'. The kettle itself is able to teach patience in this case. If it is over fuelled the fire will usually be suffocated and go out.

Remember that some learning impaired people may have difficulty in knowing how hot a served drink is and it may not be appropriate to fully boil the water or their drink may need to be cooled with cold water before it is given to them.

This activity is good fun and people gain great satisfaction and a sense of achievement in using a fire steel to light a fire. Whatever the ability of the group they can all be involved in some part of the process. All present are rewarded at the end of the activity with a hot drink.

ACTIVITY 5: FIRE

Suitable for: All ages and abilities

Resources: Fire steel, tinder, bucket of water

Benefits:

- Building fires are a good way to encourage cooperation between members of the group.

- Fuelling fires encourages patience and turn taking.

- Fires contain strong sensory stimuli, which can help to meet sensory needs – particularly visual and olfactory.

- Some learners will enjoy the process of building the structure of a fire.

- Sitting around a fire together is a bonding experience. Sharing the warmth and sensory experience does not require any additional communication to be enjoyed.

Fire holds a fascination for most people. It carries strong sensory stimuli – flickering flames, the sound of crackling, hissing and spitting logs, the warmth and the smell of woodsmoke. Fire gives a group a central focus, warmth and a means to cook. It brings many benefits to Forest School but must be treated with respect and safety procedures must be followed.

Before considering having a fire you have to make sure that it will be safely contained in the designated area, you have the means to put it out and your learners will be safe.

Site your fire pit as described in Activity 3, being aware of the danger of igniting the ground if it is peat soil or pine needles and ensuring that there is nothing around the fire or above it that could accidentally catch light.

Have a bucket of water to hand to extinguish the fire when you are finished using it or in case you have to put it out quickly.

Make sure that the group is aware of the 1.5-metre fire square or circle around the firepit.

Make sure that all learners understand not to approach the fire or cross the fire square area unless asked to do so by the person leading the session.

Consider how big a fire you need. Why are you having the fire? Cooking? Warmth? How long do you want the fire to burn for? Don't build fires that are bigger than you need.

Before lighting a fire, you need to collect your wood. Make sure that all of your wood is dead and as dry as you can find. Wood on the ground is more likely to be damp or rotten so look for standing or hanging dead wood. Remember that as dead wood breaks down it becomes a habitat for insects and fungi and be aware of sustainability and biodiversity. Don't strip all the dead wood from an area.

Collect wood of different sizes ranging from fast-burning kindling to get the fire started, to thicker logs that will burn slowly and give out a steady heat.

If the weather is wet you may consider using a billhook to split a log and putting this, split side up, as a dry base for the fire. Your logs may burn more easily if you split them before placing them on the fire. If you are not confident using a billhook then don't worry, just make your base using a row of dry sticks.

If the weather has been dry and the ground is peat or pine needles you may want to soak the area around the fire with water or use a firebowl to stop the ground from smouldering.

Light the fire using tinder and a fire steel as described in Activity 4.

When it comes to building the fire up, there are lots of different ways to do this depending on what you wish to use your fire for. Whichever type of fire you build, the basics stay the same. Remember the fire triangle: your fire needs heat, fuel and air.

Once your kindling is alight, build up the fire with wood that gradually gets thicker. A pyramid shape, or a larger version of the waffle which we use in the kelly kettle, allows that vital air to get into the fire to feed the flames. Some autistic learners will enjoy the process of building the structure of a fire and learning how this affects the efficiency with which the wood will burn.

Once your fire is lit, it must be attended at all times. An unattended fire may simply go out but it may also spread out of control or learners may run back to the fire area and need to have someone present to ensure that they behave safely.

As with all activities, you should involve your entire group lighting and fuelling your fire if it is safe to do so. If your group is able, you should be gradually withdrawing your involvement until you are standing back to observe and ensure that safety procedures are followed.

If you aren't experienced in having campfires then you should probably practise first. This is best done in the company of friends and your favourite tipple.

ACTIVITY 6: COOKING ON A FIRE

Suitable for: All ages and abilities

Resources: Fire steel, tinder, bucket of water, food, utensils (depending on how you plan to cook), tongs or fire gauntlets, handwashing soap and/or alcohol gel

Benefits: Independence, choice making, skill transference, sensory stimuli, working as a team, social interaction, communication

As with all activities, this can be as simple or complicated as you choose to make it. All manner of kit is available for outdoor cooking such as dutch ovens, trivets, tripods and quite beautiful cast-iron kettles and pots. Filling your kitbag with these beauties will be very expensive so I'd advise you to keep things simple to start with.

The easiest thing to begin cooking on a fire is probably a marshmallow on a stick. Simply peel the bark from the end of a straight stick of green wood. Hazel is ideal if it is available. Ensure that you have the landowner's permission before you cut any green wood and that you know how to do this in a manner that will not cause damage to a living tree.

Make sure the stick is long enough that you can stand far enough away from the fire. Notice how differently a marshmallow will cook if held near flames or embers. Be aware that if held near flames the marshmallow can catch light. It'll cook much better if held just above glowing embers.

Follow your fire safety procedure and only invite as many learners to the fire to cook marshmallows as you can keep safe at any one time. Make sure that people aren't waving flaming marshmallows around on the end of sticks. We're making snacks, not medieval weapons. Make sure that people let the marshmallows cool before eating. Enjoy!

Almost as easy (and much healthier!) is roasting vegetables in foil. Choose vegetables that will roast well, such as onions, mushrooms and peppers. Learners can practise cooking life skills such as peeling and chopping. Let the group prepare individual tin foil parcels. Place the veg on the foil with a splash of oil or a knob of butter. Fold the sides of the parcel and cook for 10–15 minutes on the embers at the edge of the fire. Ensure that you wear suitable fire and heat protective gloves or use tongs when placing them there. The food can be eaten straight from the foil or added to a wrap and enjoyed.

Once you are confident using fire to cook then you may want to begin to use pots and pans. The most important thing to make sure of is that your pan is balanced safely. There are different ways to do this. You may use a metal tripod and chain to hang your pan. This method allows you to hang the pan at different heights above the fire to control the heat but it is not a method I like to use in Forest School as I feel that having a pan swinging on a chain is less safe than other methods that we can just as easily use.

Beautiful horseshoe trivets are available, which stand on legs and can be positioned above whichever part of the fire you wish to use. These are really beautiful bits of kit but unless you know someone who can make them for you they are often expensive to buy.

The easiest and best value method is to take a large grill and to suspend it over the fire balanced on either side on green logs. Make sure that it is steady and can bear the weight of the cooking pots before you put them on and ensure that when you remove it you are wearing gloves and that it is put somewhere to cool where no one can touch it. Some people have fire grills made up with folding legs at each corner and these are very useful.

Whole books are written about the art of cooking outdoors and there are lots of great recipes available online. It's great fun learning to cook on a fire and I have often found that autistic learners who are reluctant to try new foods at home are more willing to have a taste of something different when they have cooked it outside.

Whenever we work with food we must ensure that we do so safely. Before even considering serving any food and drink make sure that you are aware of any medical conditions or preferences your learners may have and that nobody is left out because they cannot eat the food you've brought. The same food hygiene considerations apply outdoors as indoors and I would recommend taking an outdoor food hygiene course. My local Forest School Association group arranged a course for its members and it is inexpensive when making a group booking. The essential things to remember are to avoid cross-contamination of food by making sure that all utensils are clean and are stored in a way that prevents them becoming dirty before being used. You should have water and soap available for regular hand washing. All food should be fresh and stored in containers which prevent it becoming cross-contaminated. Keep raw and cooked foods separate. I like to cook meat on a fire at home but choose not to do so at Forest School as some of my learners would not notice if it was undercooked and this would increase the risk of food poisoning.

Be aware of the need for risk assessments for the food preparation, particularly the use of knives to chop and the handling of hot pans and utensils. Wear heatproof gloves when handling pans that have been on the fire.

Cooking and eating together is a great social activity and is enjoyed by all members of my groups. I try to ensure that we have one cooking session a month and encourage the members of the group to make choices about what we will prepare. Some people bring food from home to prepare as part of their session and choose to share it with the rest of the group. My personal favourite was fruit kebabs which were dipped in dark chocolate. We melted the chocolate in a bowl placed in a pan of water boiled over the fire. Yummy!

ACTIVITY 7: CHARCOAL MAKING

Suitable for: All ages and abilities

Resources: Sealable metal container with a hole made in the lid, fire steel, secateurs, welding gloves (fire gauntlets)

Benefits: Communication, fine motor skills, sensory stimuli, learning about fire safety

This is another activity that makes use of fire. All the safety precautions need to be in place as before. This activity is good fun and the charcoal you produce can be used in other activities.

You will need a cylindrical tin big enough to contain just as much charcoal as you need for your group. The tin will need a metal lid with a small hole made in the centre.

Collect straight pieces of green wood. Willow works well but you can use other types of wood too. They need to be about as thick as pencil and enough to fill the tin up. Trim them to size using secateurs and pack them into the tin. Can the group guess what you're going to make?

Place the tin upright in the fire using tongs or holding it between green sticks.

As the tin heats up, steam and white smoke will pour out of the hole in the lid. The smoke will turn darker as the wood inside turns into charcoal. Carefully remove the tin and cover the hole. Allow the tin to cool then remove the lid. You should have some charcoal!

Remember to involve all the group in each step of the activity. When you remove the lid, encourage the learners to smell the charcoal and then demonstrate how it can now be used to draw with.

You could try using the charcoal to carry out the leaf-rubbing activity or to make freehand drawings.

ACTIVITY 8: GO FIND IT

Suitable for: All ages and abilities

Resources: Go Find It cards

Benefits: Sensory stimuli, working as a team, social interaction, communication

The Sensory Trust is an organisation that promotes access to nature-based sensory experiences with an emphasis on inclusion. It produces a sensory card game called Go Find It, which I would recommend buying (it's available from the website).

Go Find It consists of a pack of cards, each of which describes a sensory experience. There are colours, shapes, textures, smells and a few surprises! (You'll need to buy a pack to find out what!)

The simplest way to use the cards is to take your group for a sensory walk and to fan the pack, like a magician, and ask each person to choose a card. Read the card with the learner then they must find an object that relates to the sensory word on the card. When they return with the object, explore the sensory aspects of whatever they have found before asking them to choose another card.

The game can be modified however you like. Perhaps the learners could work together in a team. Maybe they could choose several cards at a time and work their way through to find them all.

Go Find It is a great way to encourage a group to explore the sensory environment and can be a good way to give someone the opportunity to achieve if they show strength in visual tasks, as the first part of finding the objects is spotting them. With my groups, I find that the communication involved in the game is often the source of valuable observations. Learners who use limited verbal communication often surprise their support with the level at which they comprehend received communication, and Go Find It can be a great way to encourage staff to reflect on how to best communicate with the person they are supporting.

I find Go Find It to be a great resource in many ways, not least because the cards come in a small bag and can be kept to hand in a pocket and pulled out whenever you need them. They are very handy if a group has rushed through an activity and you find that you have more time left than you expected!

I make no apologies for my blatant plugging of the Sensory Trust and would encourage readers to check out its website if you haven't already.

ACTIVITY 9: DEN BUILDING

Suitable for: All ages and abilities

Resources: Depending on how you plan to make a den – string, knives, bowsaws, billhooks

Benefits: Working as a team, social interaction, communication, creativity, building structures, fine and gross motor skills, exercise

Den building is a really fun activity enjoyed by all ages. Older groups may prefer to call this activity shelter building but the principle remains the same. If you have learners who love the computer game Minecraft then this is the activity for them! You can develop this idea if the learner responds well to it. Ask them to explain Minecraft to you and try to apply the ideas of the game to the activity. It's a great way to bond with a learner as you give them the opportunity to share one of their interests with you.

Like most activities, den building can be as simple or as complicated as you want. You can build elaborate dens that involve teaching knots and lashings and make use of tools or very simple dens which use only the things which you can find in the woods.

To make a basic den you should only use dead wood and brash. Living wood can be used as part of the structure but only to lean or hang things on and should not be damaged in any way. Working out the structure is a large part of the fun of den building and you should give your learners the chance to work this out themselves. If the learners cannot do this then encourage their support staff to take the lead and involve the people they're supporting in a team effort. Some autistic learners really enjoy the challenge of building structures and become engrossed in the task. If some members of the group cannot do some aspects of the activity then make sure that you break it down into parts and allocate them the part of the task that they can achieve. Learners may enjoy finding and transporting materials, building or designing. Although people can build individual dens, this is a great activity to do in a group as it encourages cooperation to achieve a shared goal, turn taking, communication and compromise.

I am deliberately not giving you a template for den design. Remember that this is not bushcraft or a survival challenge. We aren't going to rely on these dens to shelter us through a night of storms in a barren wilderness. It doesn't matter if the group produces a palace or a few sticks leant against a tree. This activity is about the process rather than the product. Help the group if they are struggling but otherwise stand back and observe, encourage and praise.

You may want to introduce tool use to this session. The safe use of tools is covered in Chapter 8. Remember that each tool needs to be individually risk assessed and that some learners may require person-specific risk assessments. You may wish to cut some branches to size using a bowsaw. Always introduce the bowsaw by giving a safety talk as described in Chapter 8 and ensure that learners are closely supervised and everyone is following the safe handling procedures correctly.

You can elaborate on this activity if you like by introducing small challenges. Can a group make some type of door knocker or perhaps a doormat? Is the den rainproof? Perhaps you could test this by getting a member of staff to sit inside while a learner sprinkles the roof with a watering can!

When observing den building be aware of whether the den's structure is safe. Make sure it isn't likely to collapse on people and that there are no sharp points sticking out which people may injure themselves on. Make sure that people carry branches safely with the point facing the ground and not waving around at eye level. Challenge yourself to avoid saying, 'You'll have someone's eye out with that!'

Make sure that learners remain within the agreed boundaries of your site and that you are aware of their whereabouts at all times when they are collecting materials to build with.

Den building is great fun. If you have the landowner's permission and the structure is safe, a den can be left up. Some autistic learners may wish to use a den, whether built by the individual or by a group, as a quiet place to retreat to if they need space. It can be good to involve some learners in choosing and building this space themselves to promote a feeling of ownership and to encourage them to consider how to make it to their own specifications to accommodate their needs.

ACTIVITY 10: GYPSY FURNITURE

Suitable for: More experienced groups

Resources: Bowsaw, loppers, hammer, nails, billhook, strike

Benefits: Working as a team, social interaction, communication, creativity, building structures, fine and gross motor skills, exercise

This activity can be carried out by all ages and abilities but younger children or people with more severe impairments will need close supervision and support. Tool use should have been introduced gradually in previous sessions before attempting this type of project.

Gypsy furniture is traditionally made from hazel or willow and makes use of green wood which has been coppiced or pollarded. Before cutting any living wood make sure that you have the permission of the landowner. If you are lucky, someone may have cut hazel or willow that you can use. If you have permission to cut your own then ensure that you know how to do this correctly and do not harm the living tree. I am not going to offer instruction on how to do this as it is better for you to find someone to give you hands-on advice to make sure you do this correctly. The landowner may employ someone to manage the woods who could show you or you may meet someone through the Forest School Association who could teach you. Choose what you are going to make – a bench, a chair or a table. Decide on the dimensions and work out how you will build the basic frame.

You will need four legs; choose wood about as thick as your wrist and cut to about 40cm long.

Decide how long and how wide your furniture will be. Cut pieces to size using a bowsaw. You will need four length pieces and four width pieces. Nail the width pieces to the sides of two legs. One near the top, the other near the bottom.

Now join the legs lengthways by nailing the end of two length pieces into the top of the legs. I cut a half lap joint onto the length piece that is being placed on top of the leg. This is done by cutting halfway through the length piece then splitting down using a billhook and strike. Nail the other two length pieces to the outside of the legs near the bottom, front and back.

You should now have a basic frame. Make it more solid by measuring diagonals between opposite sides and cutting lengths to nail in place.

Now take straight pieces of wood as thick as your thumb and place them between the back and front length pieces, nailing them at either end. Continue across until you have covered the entire length.

If you wanted a table then you're finished!

If you want a bench or chair then choose some pieces of hazel with branches that splay out. Cut to about 120cm and nail to the top and bottom length pieces. Now take supple pieces of hazel as thick as a finger and nail the thicker end to the back of the back leg and bend and weave in an arc around the splayed branches. Build these up coming from both sides until you have made a woven arc across the back of the bench.

You can create all sorts of wonderful natural shapes and contours and the furniture you make will have a natural beauty. You do not need to be a carpenter to make this furniture and a certain degree of trial and error is involved.

Make sure that all tools are risk assessed and that the group is briefed and monitored to ensure safe tool use at all times.

Resources

Forest School

Books

Some of these books concentrate mainly on Forest School provision for younger children but are still relevant in explaining Forest School approaches for other types of learner.

Constable, K. (2014) *The Outdoor Classroom in Practice, Ages 3–7. A Month-by-Month Guide to Forest School Provision.* New York, NY: Routledge.

Houghton, P. and Worroll, J. (2016) *Play the Forest School Way.* London: Watkins Media Limited.

Knight, S. (2011) *Forest School for All.* London: Sage Publications.

Knight, S. (2011) *Risk and Adventure in Early Years Outdoor Play: Learning from Forest Schools.* London: Sage Publications.

Knight, S. (2013) *International Perspectives on Forest School.* London: Sage Publications.

Knight, S. (2013) *Forest School and Outdoor Learning in the Early Years.* London: Sage Publications.

Knight, S. (2016) *Forest School in Practice.* London: Sage Publications.

Louv, R. (2010) *Last Child in the Woods: Saving our Children from Nature Deficit Disorder.* Chapel Hill, NC: Algonquin Books.

Milchem, K. and Doyle, J. (2012) *Developing a Forest School in Early Years Provision.* London: Practical Preschool Books.

Williams-Siegfredsen, J. (2017) *Understanding the Danish Forest School Approach.* New York, NY: Routledge.

Activities

There are many books available which cover outdoor activities and bushcraft. These are some of my favourites when planning activities to offer my groups.

Danks, F. and Schofield, J. (2012) *The Stick Book.* London: Francis Lincoln Ltd.

Harrison, P. (2017) *Making Woodland Crafts.* Stroud: Hawthorn Press.

MacIver, T. (2013) *Activities, Games and Challenges for Learning Outside the Classroom: The Teacher, Playworker, Outdoor Practitioner and Forest School Leader.* Exeter: Consultancy Education Forest Ltd.

Wills, K. (2013) *Outdoor First Aid.* Caernarfon: Pesda Press.

Online

The internet is a great resource for activity planning and for networking with other Forest School practitioners. The Forest School Association website can be found at: www.forestschoolassociation.org.

Sources of activities:

Forest Schooled: www.forestschooled.com

Forestry Commission England: www.forestry.gov.uk/england-learning

Pinterest: www.pinterest.co.uk

The Sensory Trust: www.sensorytrust.org.uk

The Woodland Trust: www.woodlandtrust.org.uk/naturedetectives

I highly recommend Muddy Faces as a supplier of equipment and advice: www.muddyfaces.co.uk.

Autism

There is a great deal of information available about autism in print and online. Understanding of autism continues to develop and autistic people continue to articulate their experience. The following are some suggestions of places readers who are unfamiliar with autism may start:

Attwood, T. (2007, 2015) *The Complete Guide to Asperger's Syndrome.* Philadelphia, London: Jessica Kingsley Publishers.

Baron-Cohen, S. (2008) *Autism and Asperger's Syndrome: The Facts.* Oxford: Oxford University Press.

Bogdashina, O. (2003) *Sensory Perceptual Issues in Autism and Asperger Syndrome: Different Sensory Experiences Different Prerceptual World.* Philadelphia, London: Jessica Kingsley Publishers.

Bogdashina, O. (2005) *Communication Issues in Autism and Asperger Syndrome: Do We Speak the Same Language?* Philadelphia, London: Jessica Kingsley Publishers.

Caldwell, P. (2006) *Finding You Finding Me.* Philadelphia, London: Jessica Kingsley Publishers.

Grandin, T. (2013) *The Autistic Brain: Exploring the Strength of a Different Kind of Mind.* London: Ebury Publishing.

Higashida, N. (2007, 2013) *The Reason I Jump.* London: Hodder and Stoughton.

Jackson, L. (2002) *Freaks, Geeks and Asperger Syndrome.* Philadelphia, London: Jessica Kingsley Publishers.

Silberman, S. (2015) *Neurotribes: The Legacy of Autism and How to Think Smarter About People Who Think Differently.* London: Allen & Unwin.

Online

The Middletown Centre for Autism Research Bulletins: www.middletownautism.com/research/research-bulletins

Musings of an Aspie: https://musingsofanaspie.com

The National Autistic Society: www.autism.org.uk

Network Autism: http://network.autism.org.uk

Wrong Planet (Autism Self-Advocacy Forum): http://wrongplanet.net

Notes

Chapter 1

1. Merrick, C. (2016) 'Nature-Based Preschools Take the National Stage.' Natural Start Alliance
2. Mongeau, L. (2015) 'Preschool Without Walls.' *New York Times*, 29 December 2015
3. www.englishoutdoorcouncil.org/research.in.outdoor.learning.html
4. Louv, R. (2010) *Last Child in the Woods: Saving our Children from Nature Deficit Disorder.* Chapel Hill, NC: Algonquin Books
5. Brugha, T. *et al.* (2012) *Estimating the Prevalence of Autism Spectrum Conditions in Adults: Extending the 2007 Adult Psychiatric Morbidity Survey.* Leeds: NHS Information Centre for Health and Social Care

Chapter 2

1. Autism was originally diagnosed according to criteria described by Leo Kanner in the 1940s and was regarded as a relatively rare childhood condition. However, Lorna Wing described the triad of impairments in the 1970s and re-introduced the work of Dr Hans Asperger in 1981. Wing was the first to describe autism using the term 'spectrum' and to use the term 'Asperger's syndrome' to describe people who presented the social impairments and repetitive behaviours associated with autism but had no intellectual impairment. Hans Asperger had described children who met this profile in the 1930s in work that predated Kanner's but was largely overlooked
2. www.theguardian.com/science/2016/mar/21/autism-spectrum-has-no-clear-cut-off-point-research-suggests-nature-genetics
3. 'Neurotypical' is a term used to describe people who are not on the autism spectrum. The term originated in the autism community. It is sometimes used in a broader sense to describe people who do not have mental illness, learning disability or other conditions which are perceived as being outside typical neurology
4. Hazen, E.P. *et al.* (2014) 'Sensory symptoms in autism spectrum disorders.' *Harvard Review of Psychiatry,* 22(2), 112–124; Baranek, G. (2002) 'Efficacy of sensory and motor interventions in children with autism.' *Journal of Autism and Developmental Disorders,* 32(5), 397–422

5. Plaisted, K., Swettenham, J. and Rees, L. (1999) 'Children with autism show local precedence in a divided attention task and global precedence in a selective attention task.' *Journal of Child Psychology and Psychiatry and Allied Disciplines*, 40(5), 733–742; Rinehart, N.J., Bradshaw, J.L., Moss, S.A., Brereton, A.V. and Tonge, B.J. (2000) 'Atypical interference of local detail on global processing in high-functioning autism and Asperger's disorder.' *Journal of Child Psychology and Psychiatry and Allied Disciplines*, 41(6), 769–778; Mottron, L., Belleville, S. and Menard, E. (1999) 'Local bias in autistic subjects as evidenced by graphic tasks: Perceptual hierarchization or working memory deficit?' *Journal of Child Psychology and Psychiatry*, 40(5), 743–755

6. Baron-Cohen, S. (2008) *Autism and Asperger Syndrome.* Oxford: Oxford University Press

7. https://musingsofanaspie.com

8. An explanation of this position, written by autism rights activist Jim Sinclair, can be found at: http://autismmythbusters.com/general-public/autistic-vs-people-with-autism/jim-sinclair-why-i-dislike-person-first-language

Chapter 3

1. Capaldi, C.A. *et al.* (2015) 'Flourishing in nature: A review of the benefits of connecting with nature and its application as a wellbeing intervention.' *International Journal of Wellbeing*, 5(4), 1–16

2. The most comprehensive evidence review was carried out for Natural England. Blakesley, D., Rickinson, M. and Dillon, J. (2013) 'Engaging children on the autistic spectrum with the natural environment: Teacher insight study and evidence review.' Natural England Commissioned Reports, NECR116

3. www.sciencedaily.com/releases/2009/04/090401204241.htm

4. Muris, P., Steerneman, P., Merckelbach, H., Holdrinet, I. and Meesters, C. (1998) 'Comorbid anxiety symptoms in children with pervasive developmental disorders.' *Journal of Anxiety Disorders*, 12, 387–393

5. Tantam, D. (1991) 'Asperger Syndrome in Adulthood.' In U. Frith (ed.) *Autism and Asperger Syndrome*, pp.147–183. Cambridge: Cambridge University Press

6. Wild, G. and Jones, L.D. (2012) 'Parents Perception of Effectiveness of Sensory Diets for Children: A Multiple Case Analysis.' Available at: www.sensationalbrain.com/site/wp-content/uploads/2010/03/Research-Summary.pdf

7. www.forestry.gov.uk/website/pdf.nsf/pdf/ForestSchoolEnglandReport.pdf/$FILE/ForestSchoolEnglandReport.pdf

Chapter 4

1. Temple Grandin used this phrase when interviewed by Oliver Sacks for his book *An Anthropologist on Mars: Seven Paradoxical Tales* (1995) by Alfred A. Knopf. Wrong Planet can be found at: http://wrongplanet.net

2. Yale University (2000) 'People with autism and Asperger Syndrome process faces as objects, Yale study of brain abnormalities finds.' ScienceDaily, 21 April 2000. Available at: www.sciencedaily.com/releases/2000/04/000421083337.htm

3. www.bbc.co.uk/news/disability-37560841

4. Knight, S. (2011) *Forest School for All.* London: Sage Publications, p.3

5. Asperger, H. [1944] (1991) 'Autistic Psychopathy in Childhood.' In U. Frith (ed.) *Autism and Asperger Syndrome.* Cambridge: Cambridge University Press

6.   Attwood, T. (2007, 2015) *The Complete Guide to Asperger's Syndrome*. London, Philadelphia: Jessica Kingsley Publishers, p.72
7.   Attwood, T. (2007, 2015) *The Complete Guide to Asperger's Syndrome*. London, Philadelphia: Jessica Kingsley Publishers, p.198
8.   Louv, R. (2010) *Last Child in the Woods: Saving our Children from Nature Deficit Disorder*. Chapel Hill, NC: Algonquin Books, pp.72–73
9.   Hopkins, F. (2011) 'Removing Barriers: Getting Children with Physical Challenges into the Woods.' In S. Knight (ed.) *Forest School for All*. London: Sage Publications
10. Knight, S. (ed.) *Forest School for All*. London: Sage Publications, p.100
11. Knight, S. (ed.) (2011) *Forest School for All*. London: Sage Publications, p.395
12. Grandin, T. and Panek, R. (2013) *The Autistic Brain: Exploring the Strength of a Different Kind of Mind*. New York, NY: Random House
13. Cree, J. (2014) 'The Learner Centred Principle.' Available at: www.forestschoolassociation. org/wiki/learning-and-development/learning-theoriestheorists-home-page-do-not-alter/the-learner-centred-principle-by-jon-cree-fsa-chair (members only access)

Chapter 5

1.   Attwood, T. (2015) *The Complete Guide to Asperger's Syndrome*. Philadelphia, London: Jessica Kingsley Publishers, p.142
2.   Attwood, T. (2015) *The Complete Guide to Asperger's Syndrome*. Philadelphia, London: Jessica Kingsley Publishers, pp.253–255
3.   Grandin, T. and Panek, R. (2013) *The Autistic Brain*. New York, NY: Random House, pp.89–90
4.   Attwood, T. (2015) *The Complete Guide to Asperger's Syndrome*. Philadelphia, London: Jessica Kingsley Publishers, p.289
5.   Bogdashina, O. (2005) *Communication Issues in Autism and Asperger's Syndrome*. Philadelphia, London: Jessica Kingsley Publishers, p.79
6.   Attwood, T. (2015) *The Complete Guide to Asperger's Syndrome*. Philadelphia, London: Jessica Kingsley Publishers, p.236
7.   Grey, C. (2015) *The New Social Story Book*. Arlington, TX: Future Horizons Firm
8.   Bogdashina, O. (2005) *Communication Issues in Autism and Asperger Syndrome*. Philadelphia, London: Jessica Kingsley Publishers, Chapter 6

Chapter 6

1.   Cree, J. (2014) 'The Learner Centred Principle.' Available at: www. forestschoolassociation.org/wiki/learning-and-development/learning-theoriestheorists-home-page-do-not-alter/the-learner-centred-principle-by-jon-cree-fsa-chair (members only access)
2.   Fjortoft, I. (2004) 'Landscape as playscape: The effects of natural environments on children's play and motor development.' *Children, Youth and Environments, 14,* 21–44
3.   Fjortoft, I. and Sageie, J. (2000) 'The natural environment as a playground for children: Landscape description and analysis of a natural landscape.' *Landscape and Urban Planning, 48,* 83–97
4.   Bixler, R.D., Floyd, M.E. and Hammutt, W.E. (2002) 'Environmental socialization: Qualitative tests of the childhood play hypothesis.' *Environment and Behavior, 34,* 795

5. Interview with Professor Connie Kasari (2016) *Autism and Play* Vol 2, Middletown Centre for Autism, p.6

6. Attwood, T. (2015) *The Complete Guide to Asperger's Syndrome.* Philadelphia, London: Jessica Kingsley Publishers, p.79

7. Attwood, T. (2015) *The Complete Guide to Asperger's Syndrome.* Philadelphia, London: Jessica Kingsley Publishers, p.187

8. Kasari, C. *et al.* (2012) 'Longitudinal Follow-up of children with autism receiving targeted interventions on joint attention and play.' *Journal of the American Academy of Child & Adolescent Psychiatry,* 51(5), 487–495

9. San Francisco State University (2014) 'Integrated play groups help children with autism.' ScienceDaily. 27 October 2014. Available at: www.sciencedaily.com/releases/2014/10/141027182950.htm

10. Wolfberg, P., DeWitt, M., Young, G.S. and Nguyen, T. (2014) 'Integrated play groups: Promoting symbolic play and social engagement with typical peers in children with ASD across settings.' *Journal of Autism and Developmental Disorders,* 45(3)

11. www.teacch.com

12. www.scerts.com

13. Caldwell, P. (2013) Network Autism article. Available at: http://network.autism.org.uk/knowledge/insight-opinion/top-5-tips-autism-professionals-using-intensive-interaction (members only access)

14. Caldwell, P. (2013) Network Autism article. Available at: http://network.autism.org.uk/knowledge/insight-opinion/top-5-tips-autism-professionals-using-intensive-interaction (members only access)

15. Mills, R. (2016) 'Reflections on stress and autism.' Network Autism article. Available at: http://network.autism.org.uk/good-practice/evidence-base/reflections-stress-and-autism (members only access)

16. Wetherby, A.M. and Prizant, B.M. (1992) 'Facilitating language and communication development in autism: Assessment and intervention guidelines.' In D.E. Berkell (ed.) *Autism: Identification, Education and Treatment.* Hillsdale, NJ: Lawrence Erlbaum Publishers

17. www.autism.org.uk/about/what-is/pda.aspx

Chapter 7

1. Leekam, S.R., Nieto, C., Libby, S.J., Wing, L. and Gould J. (2007) 'Describing the sensory abnormalities of children and adults with autism.' *Journal of Autism and Developmental Disorders,* 37, 894–910

2. Bogdashina, O. (2014) Network Autism. Available at: http://network.autism.org.uk/knowledge/insight-opinion/top-5-tips-autism-professionals-dr-olga-bogdashina-sensory-difficulties (Members only access)

Chapter 8

1. Louv, R. (2010) *Last Child in the Woods: Saving our Children from Nature Deficit Disorder.* Chapel Hill, NC: Algonquin Books

Index